AN ADULT COLORING BOOK FOR CAT LOVERS

SPECIALS CATS & HILARIOUS SCENES

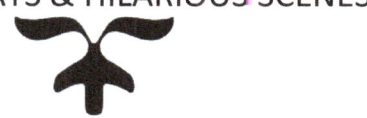

AÑO 2020
VOLUME 2
MRS. GLADYS VALENCIA

Presentation

For me, cats are little beings that bring light into our lives. Just by stroking them, our problems feel small. Just by looking at them and our fears disappear. They are magical beings that when they enter our lives flood him with joy. One has not known happiness without having lived with a cat. So I want to dedicate the art of relaxation through coloring cats, who give us so much love in our lives.

There are 35 drawings of cats different from each other, in fun situations. They are designed so that the background can be completed with more drawings and expand your creativity in each proposal.

They are not so ornate shapes, ideal for adults or for any cat lover of any age with a lot of creativity and a desire to express themselves through color.

Enjoy it !!

Mrs. Gladys Valencia

The life you deserve to live.

The best tips and digital resources that I recommend to improve your quality of life and well-being.

Foolw us !!

Facebook: www.facebook.com/romeo101.hack.your.life
Instagram: @romeo101.hack.your.life

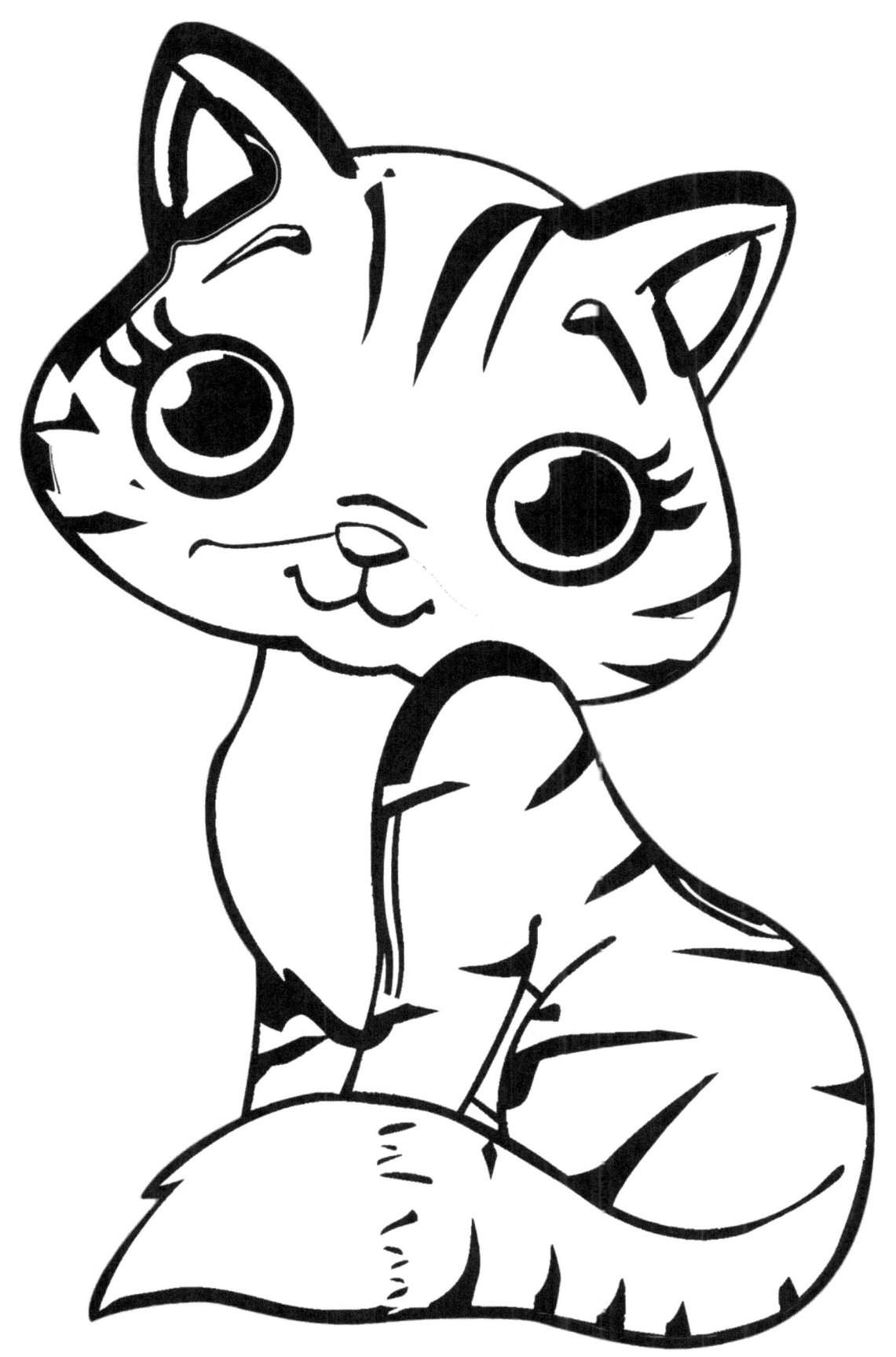

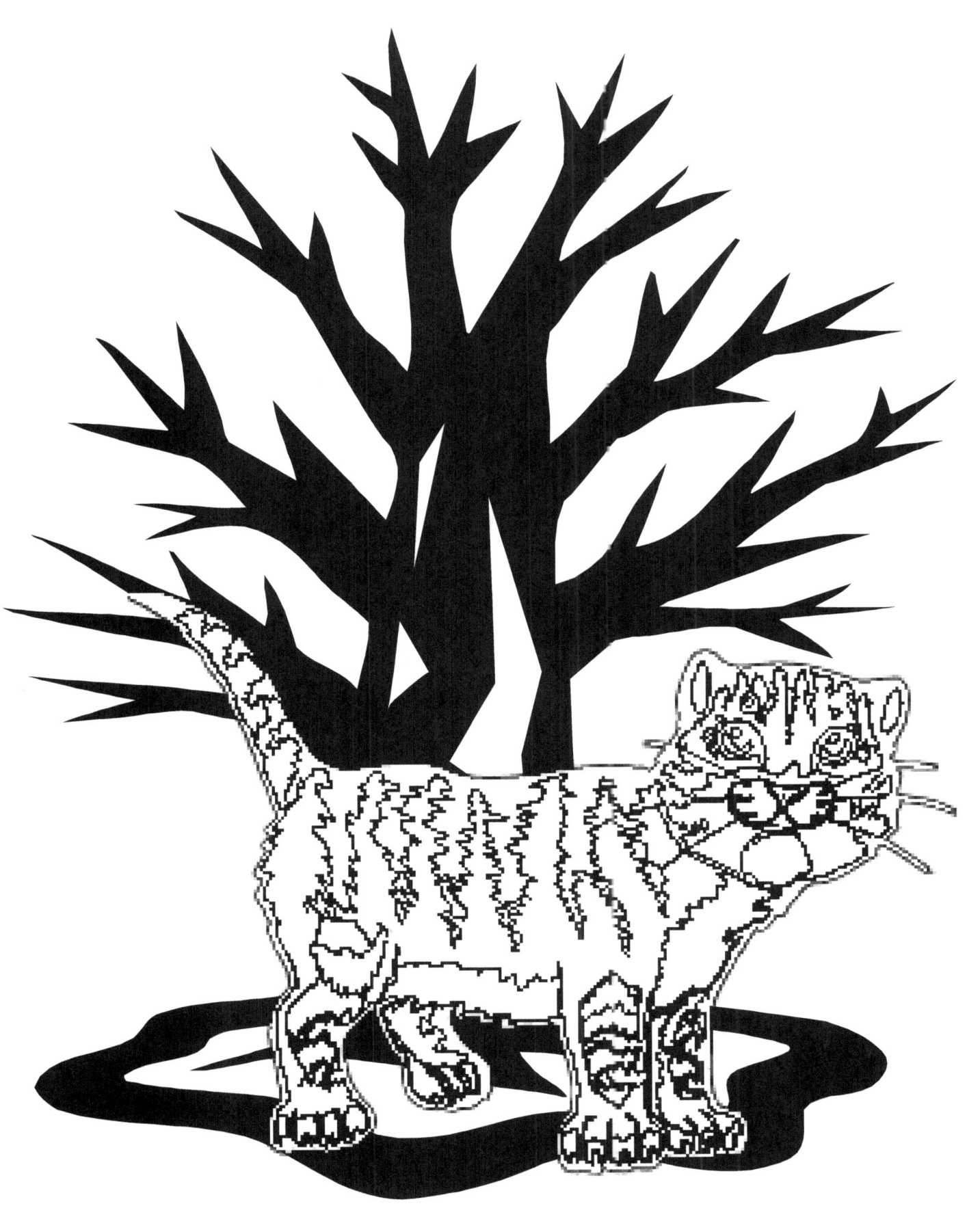

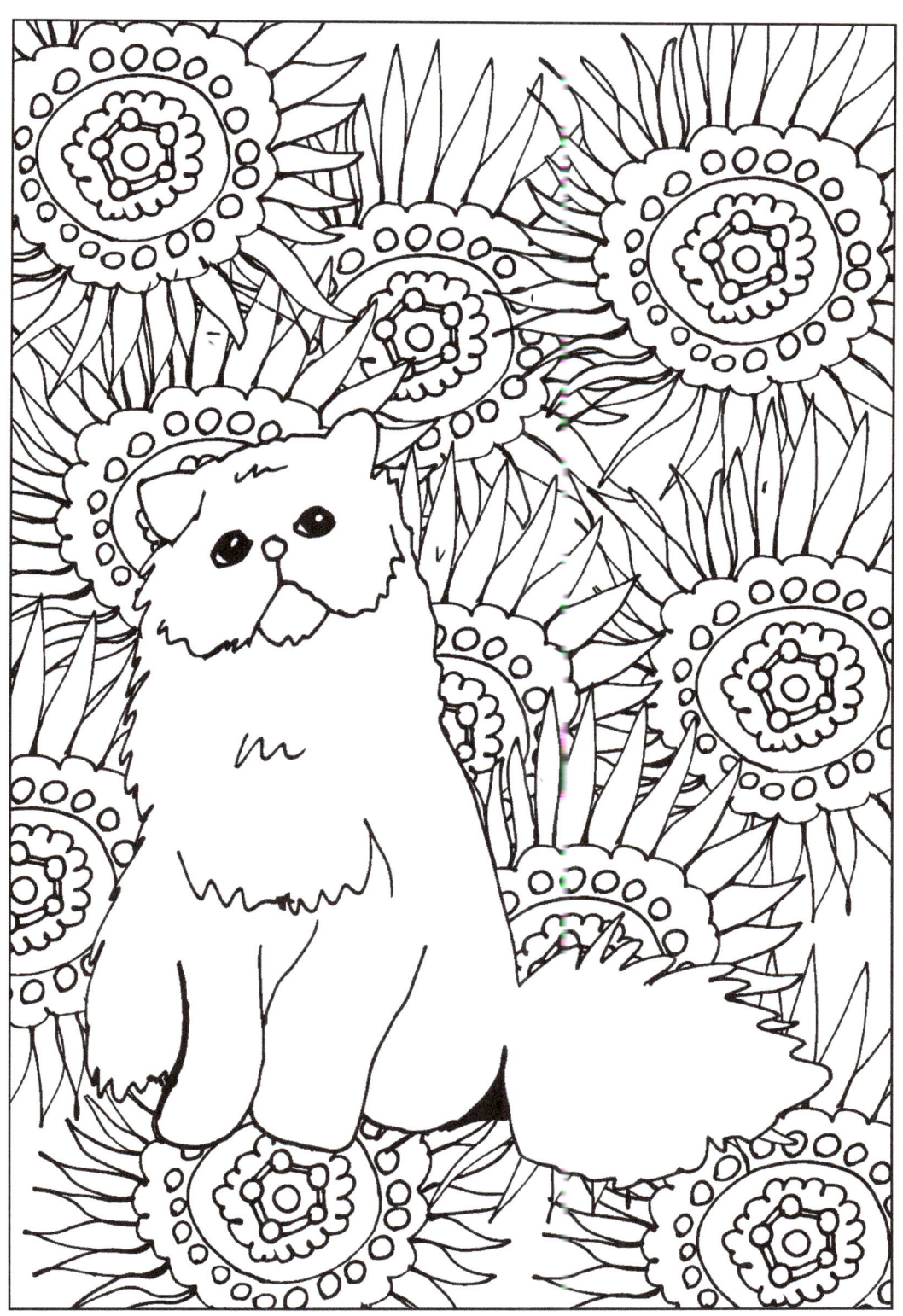

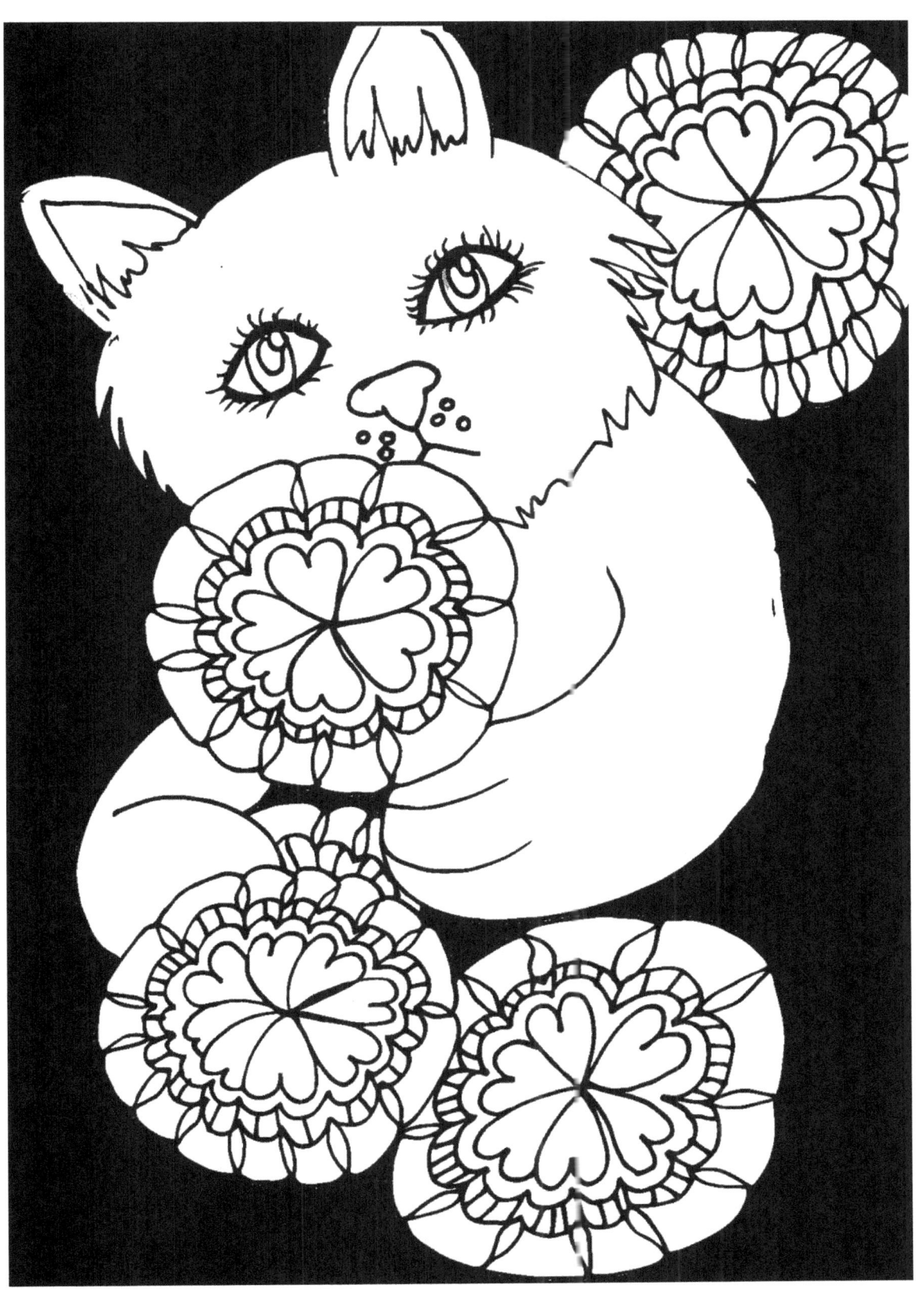

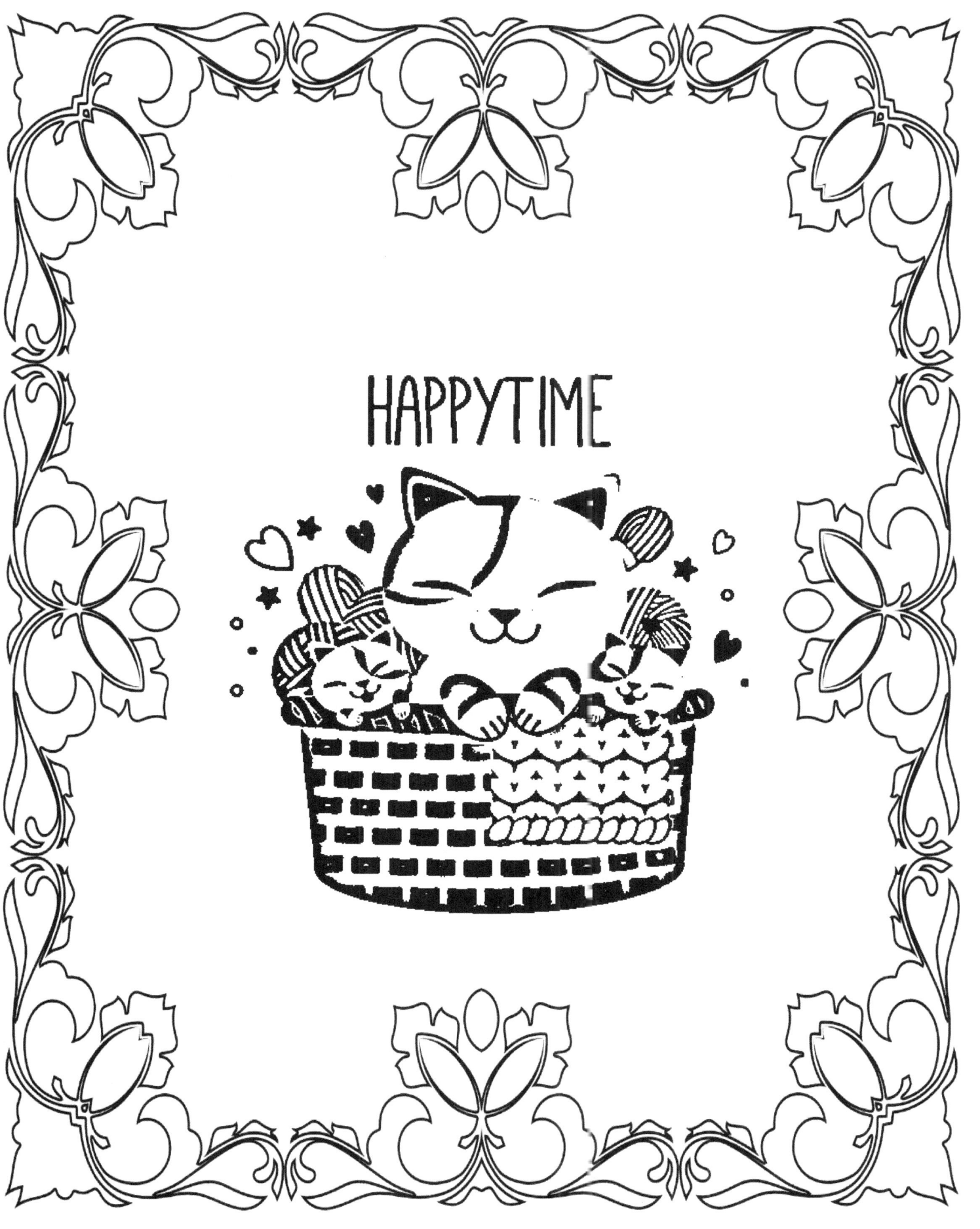

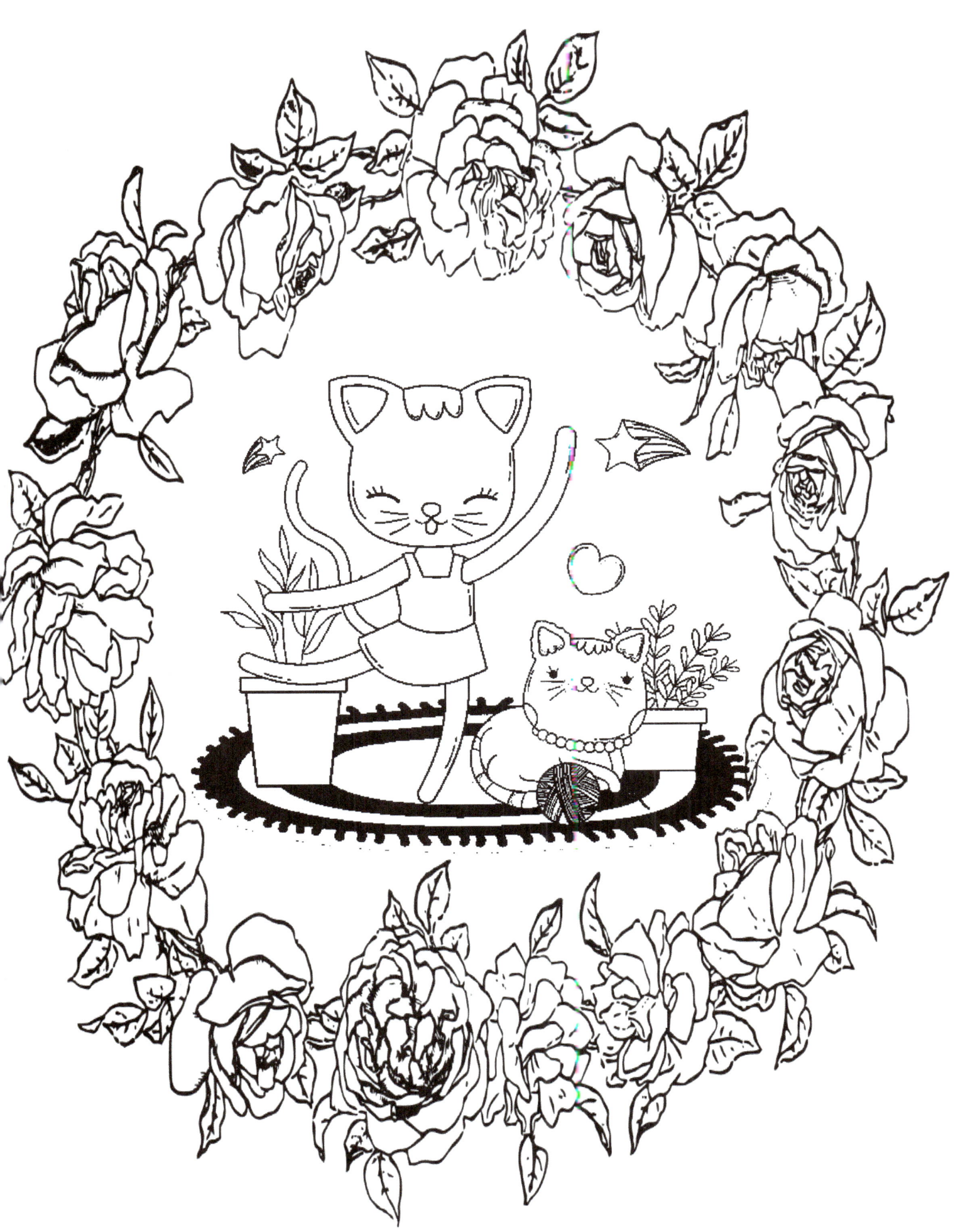

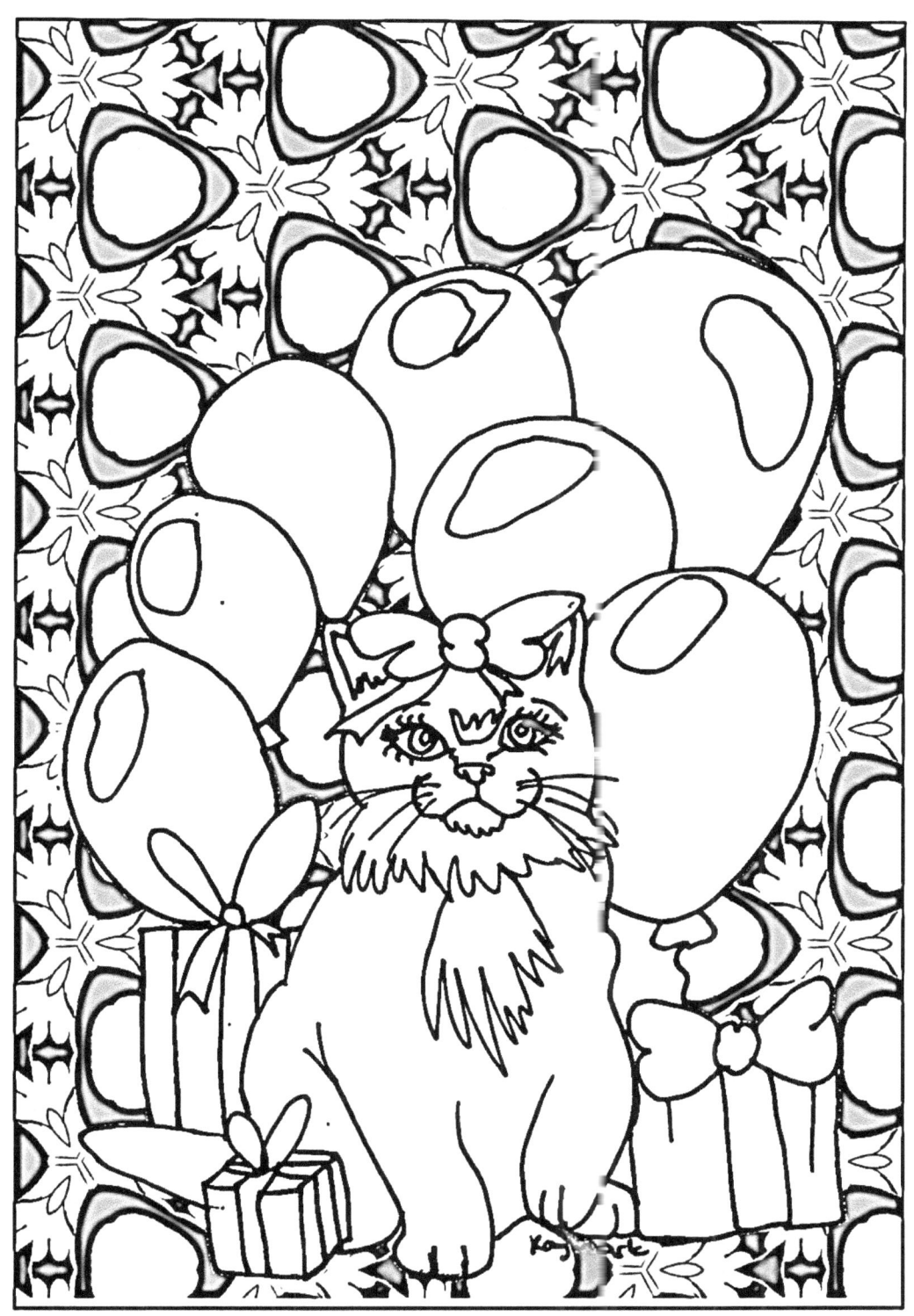

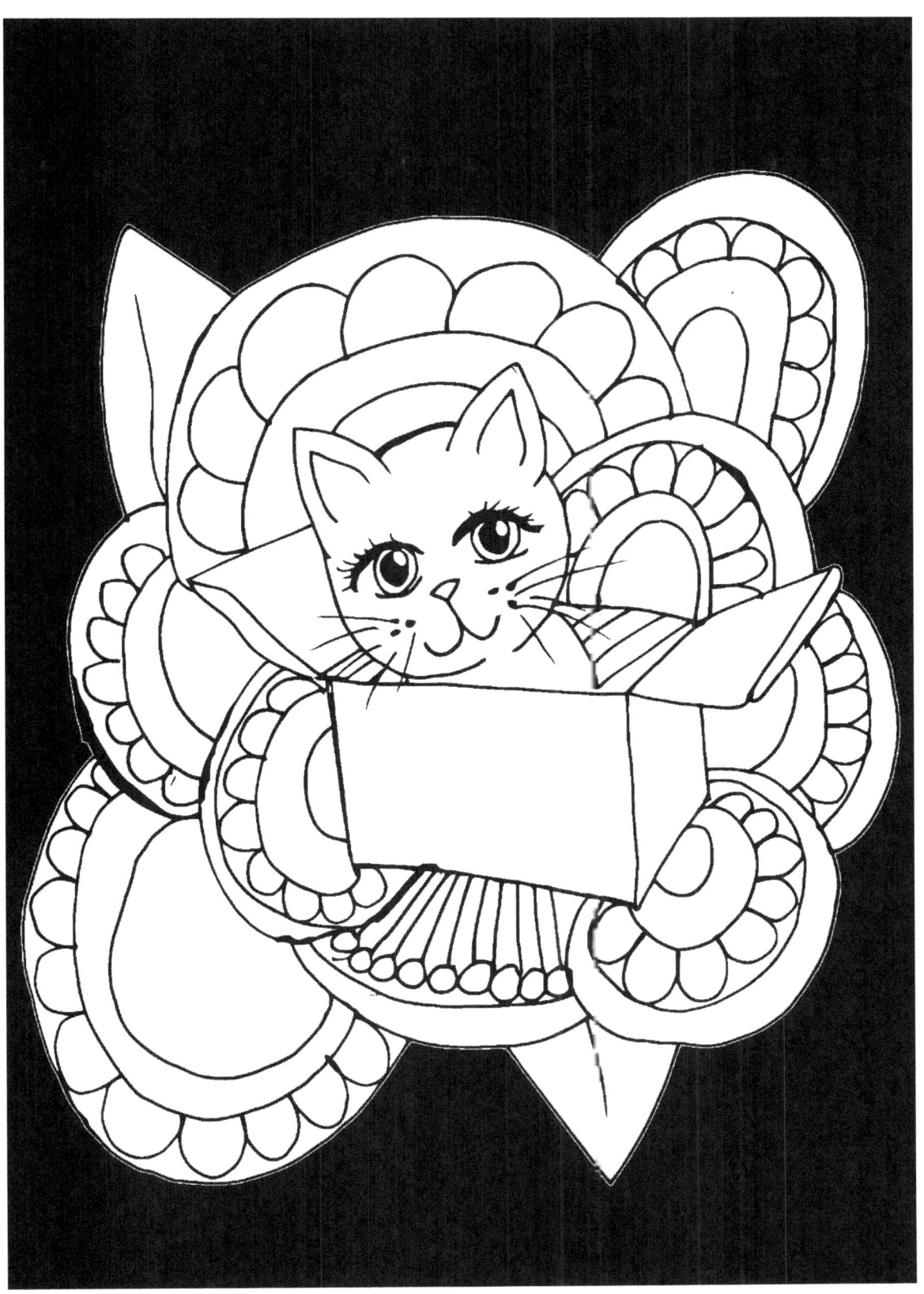

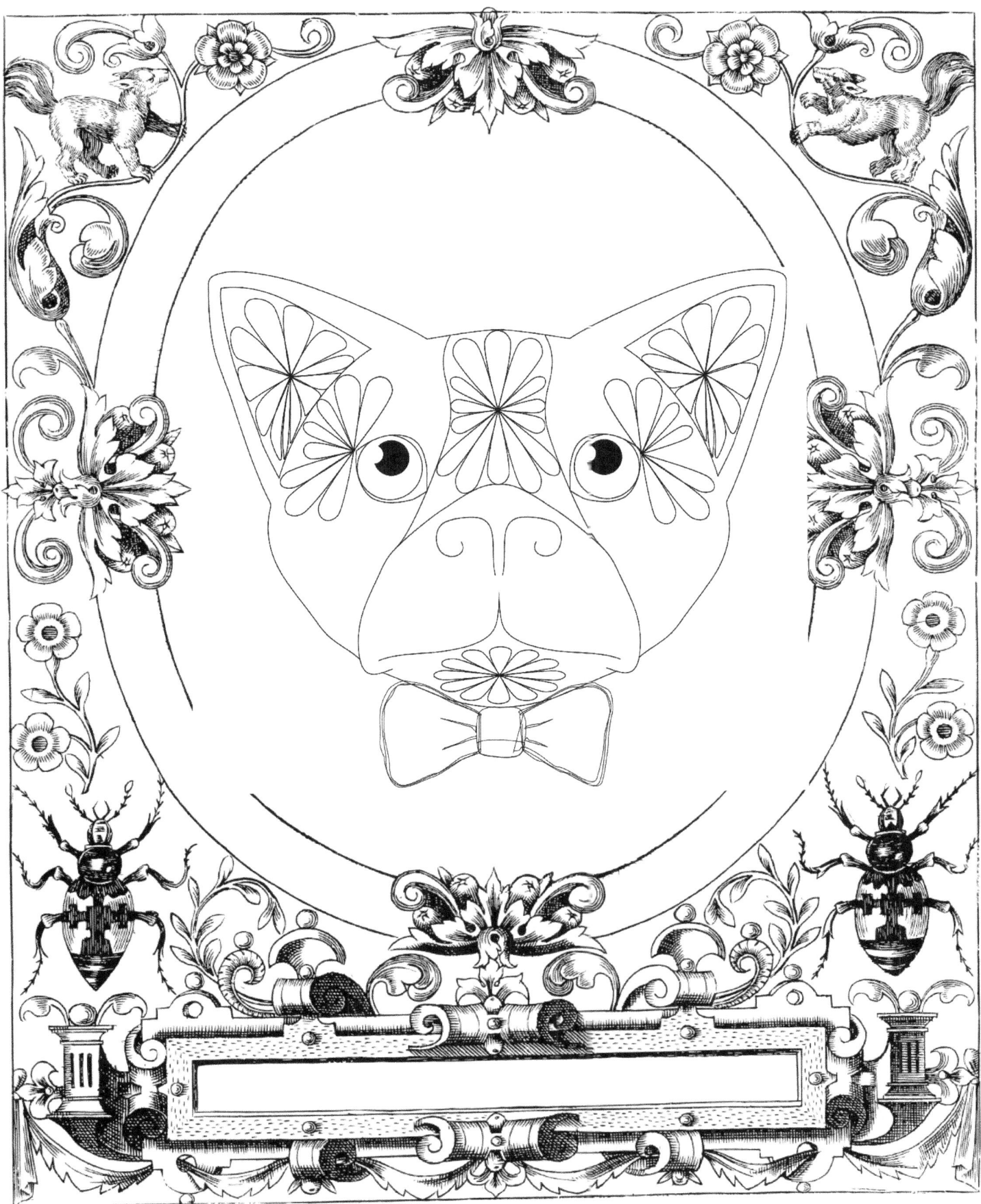

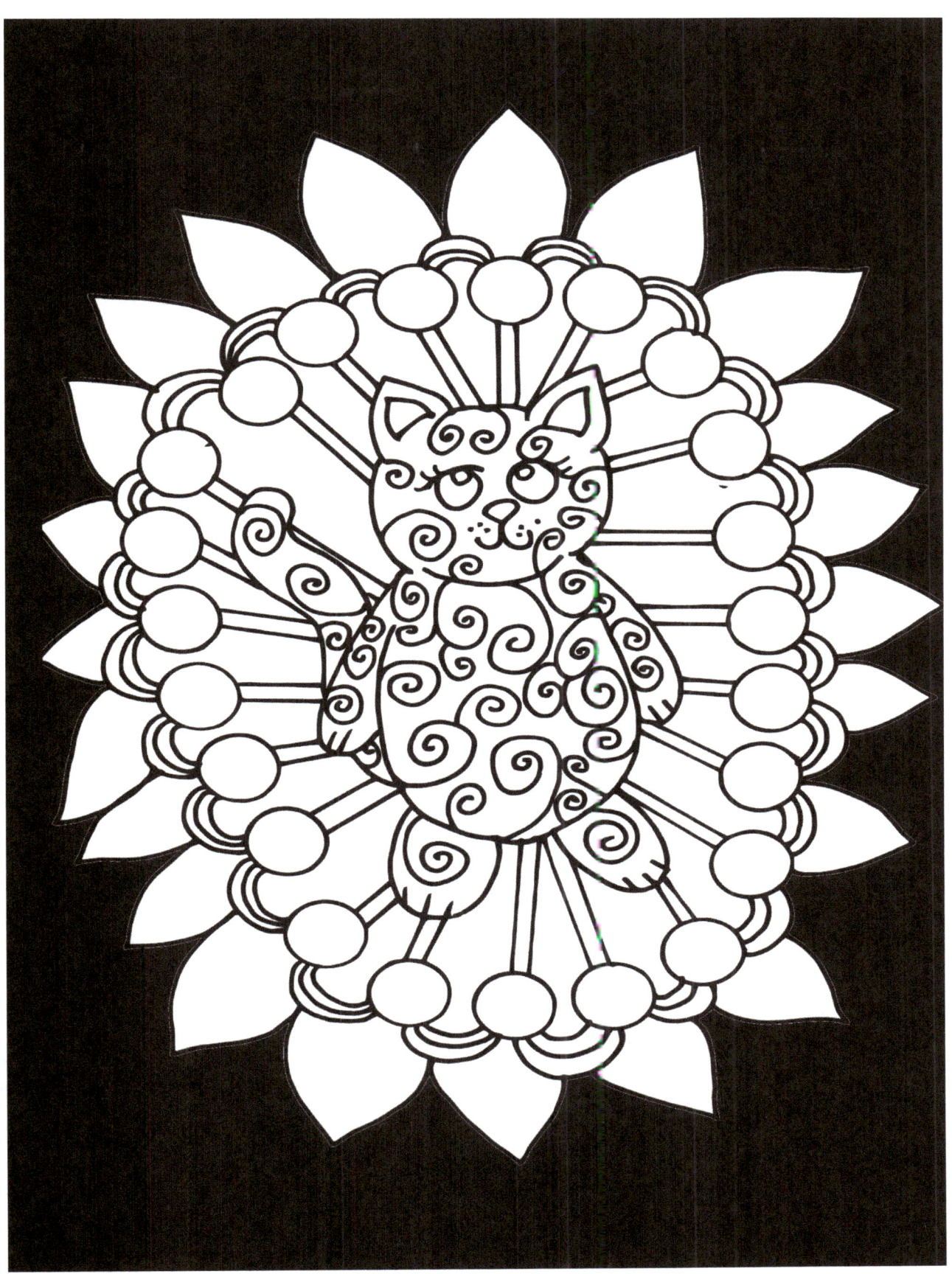

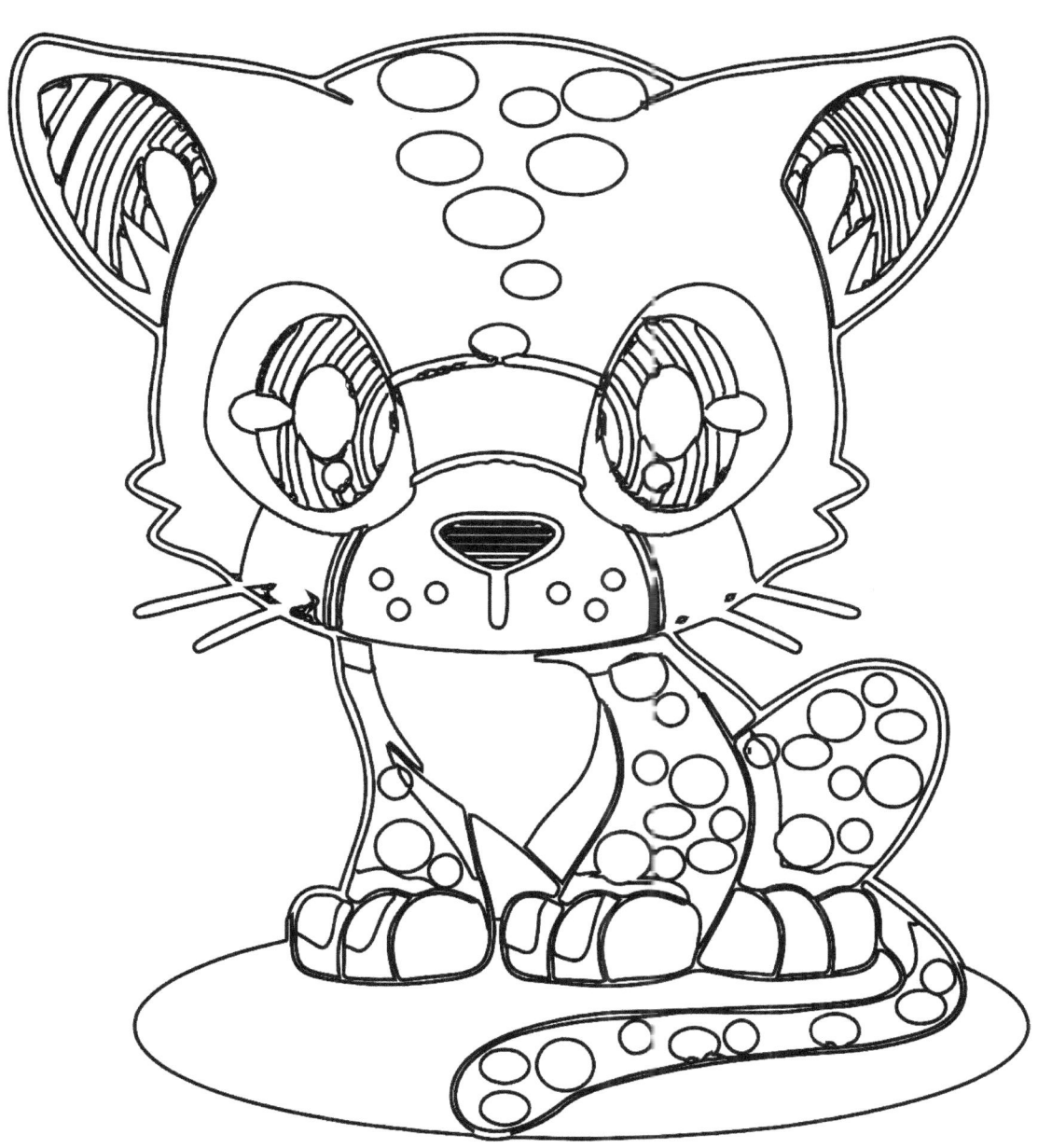

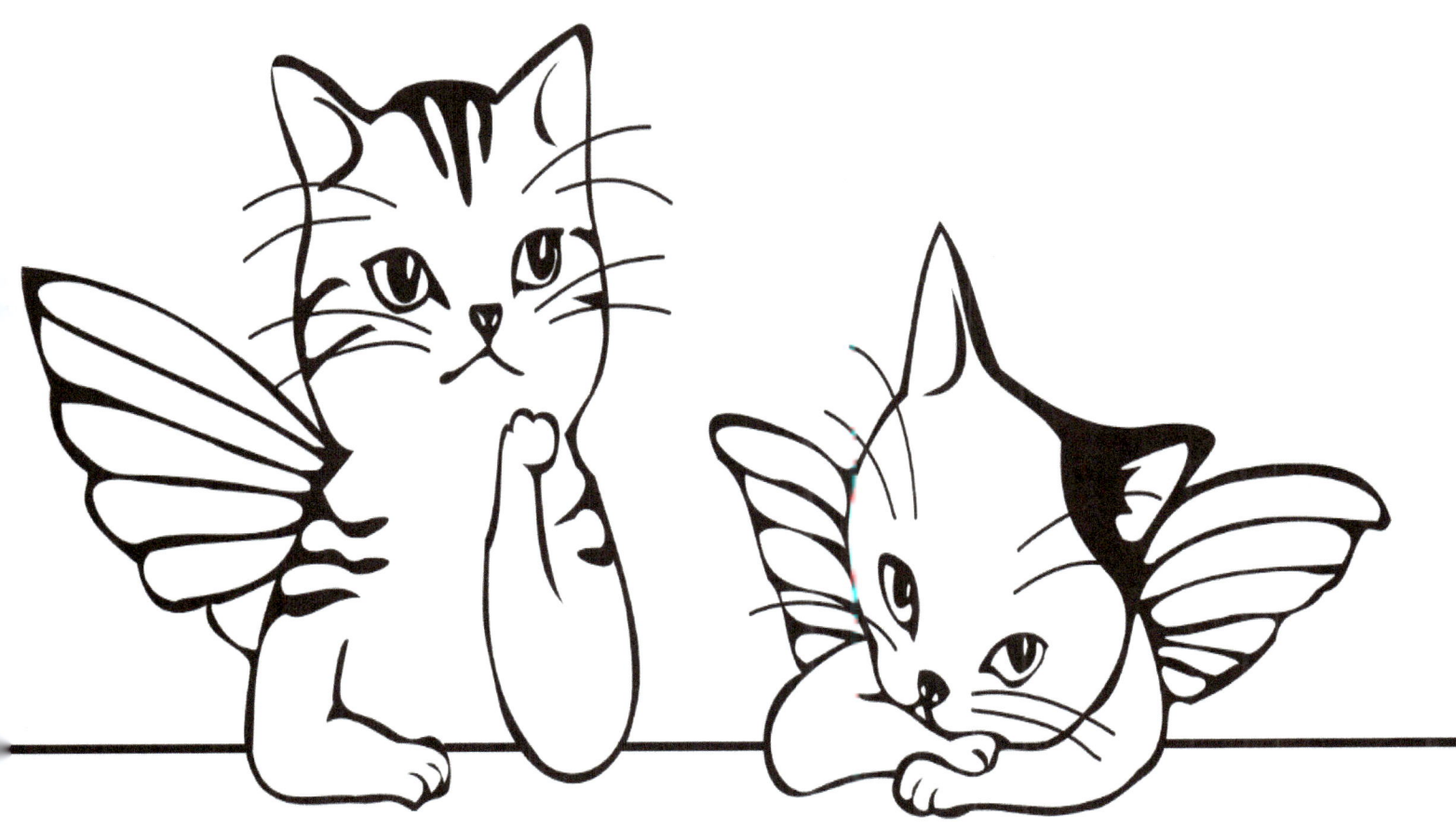

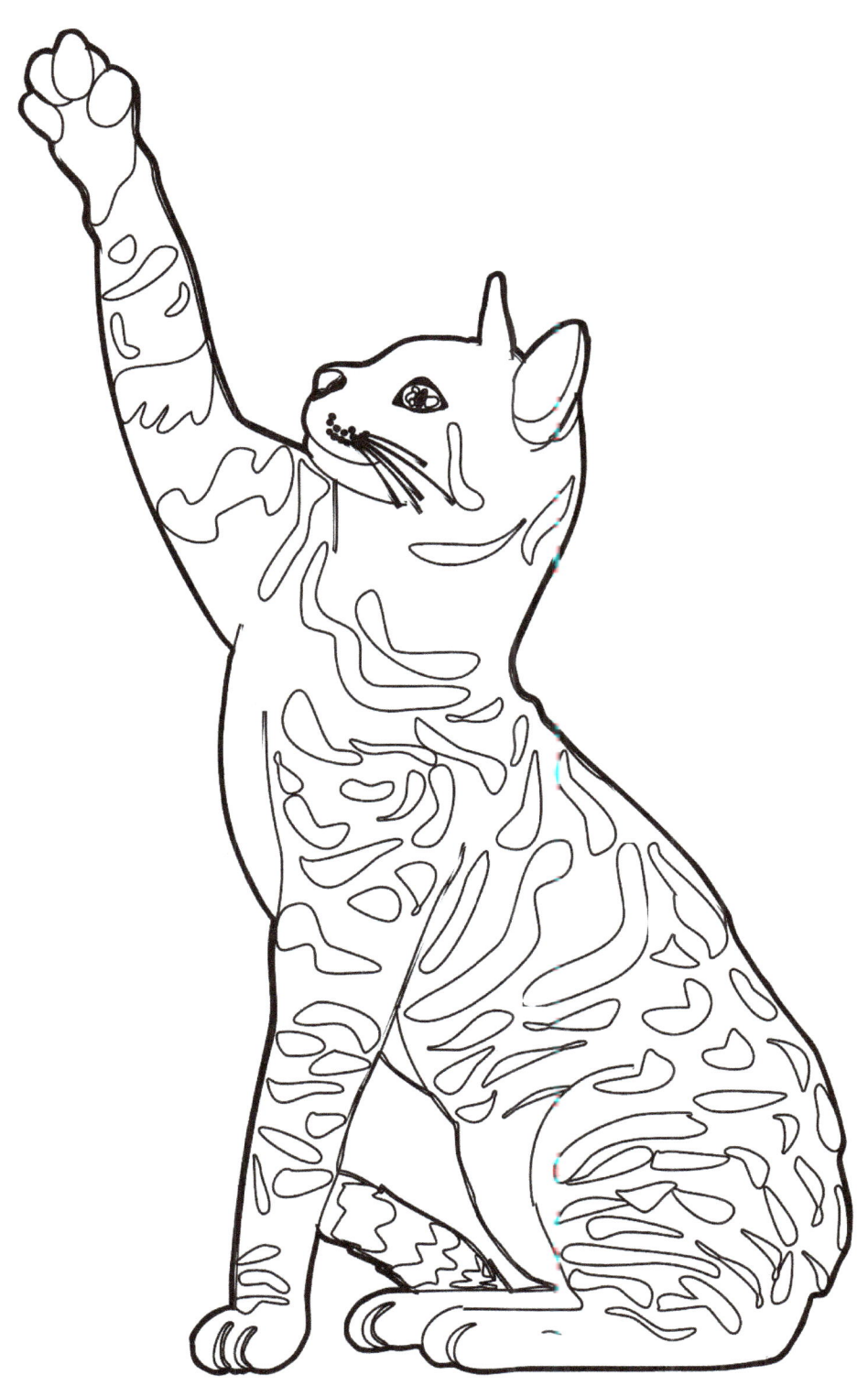

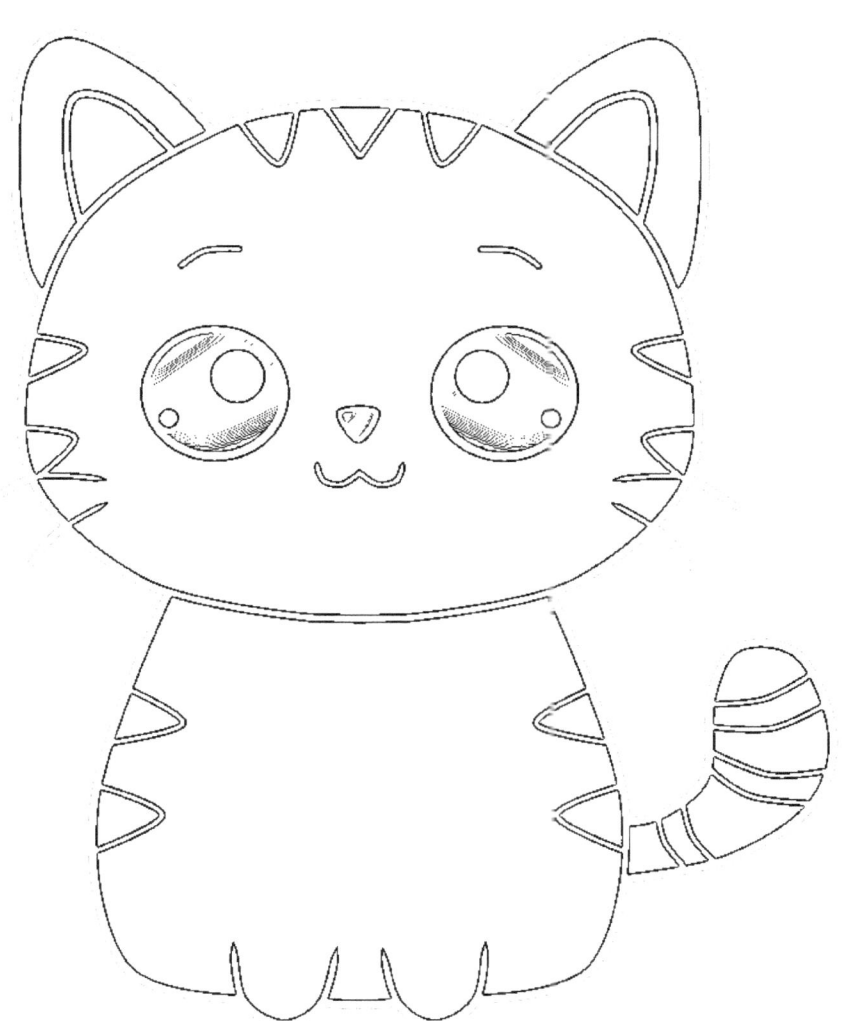

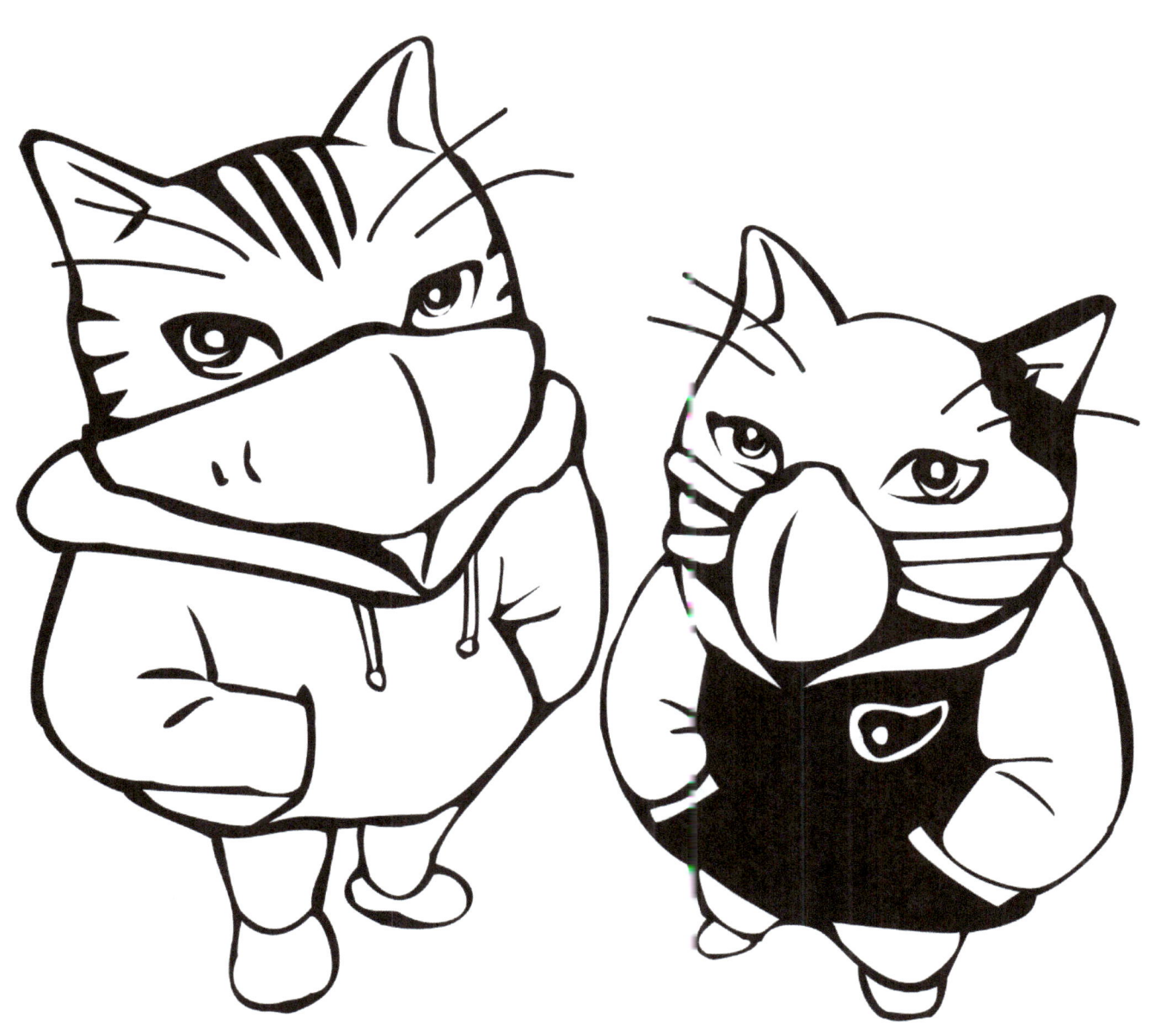

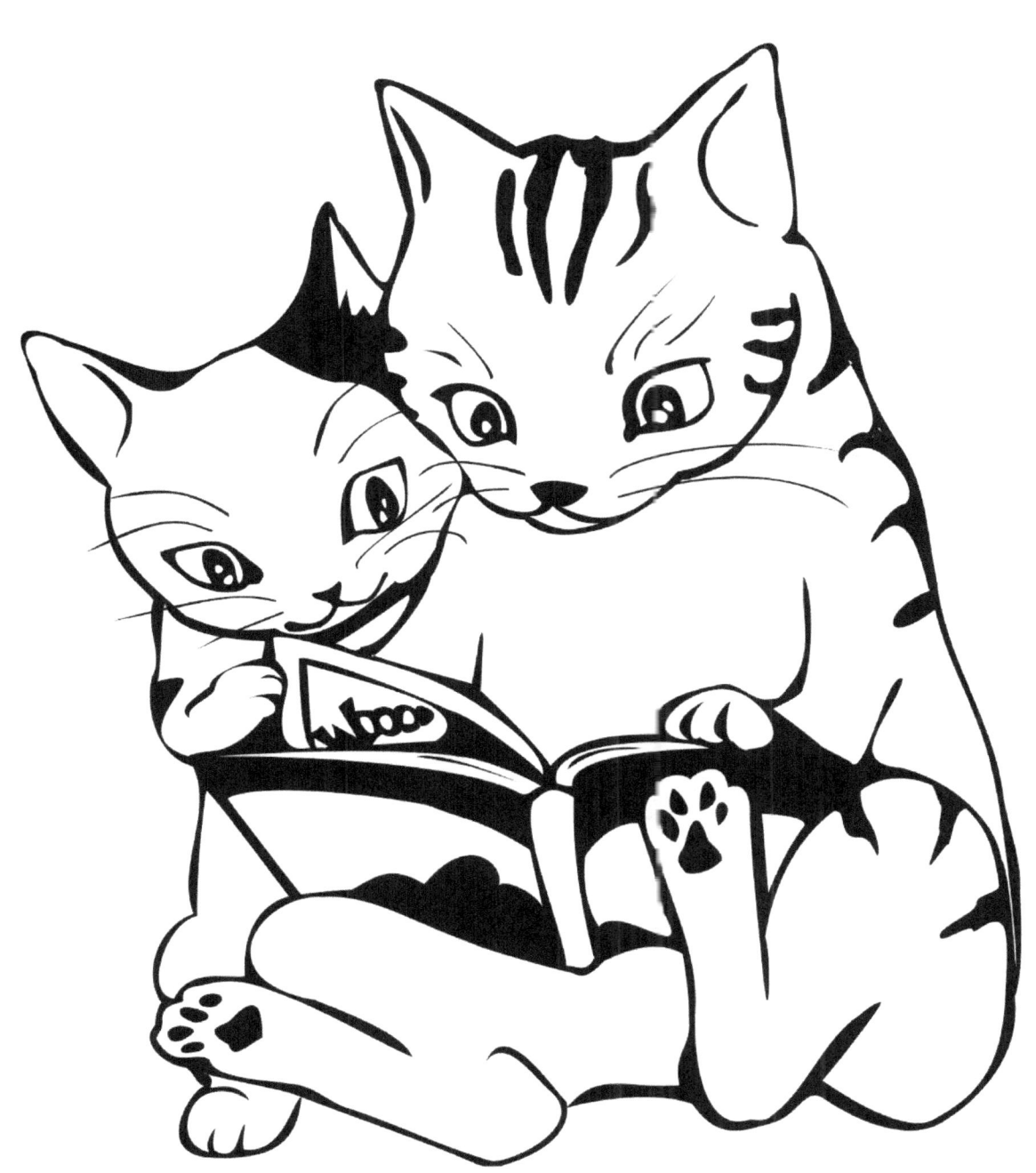

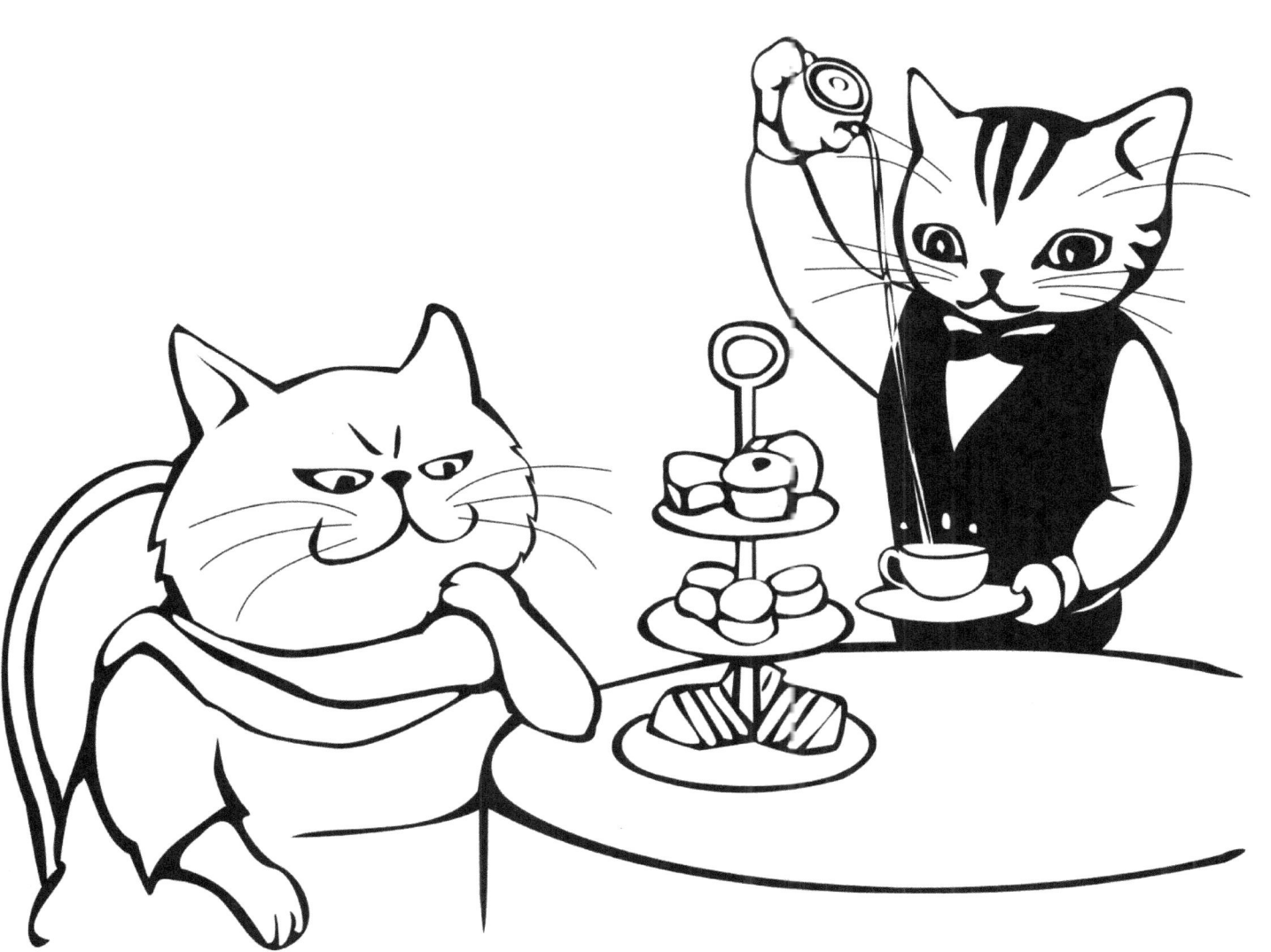

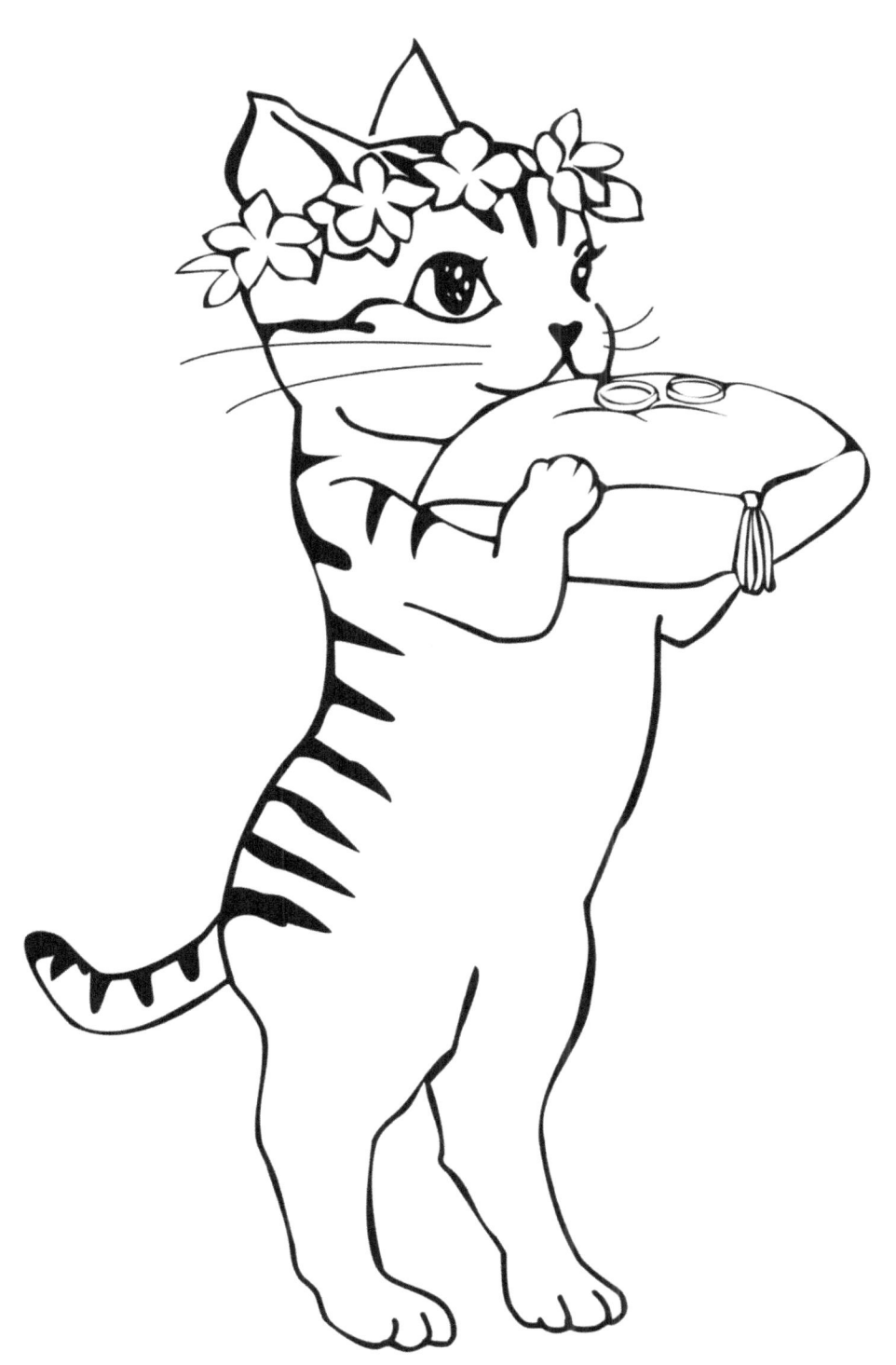

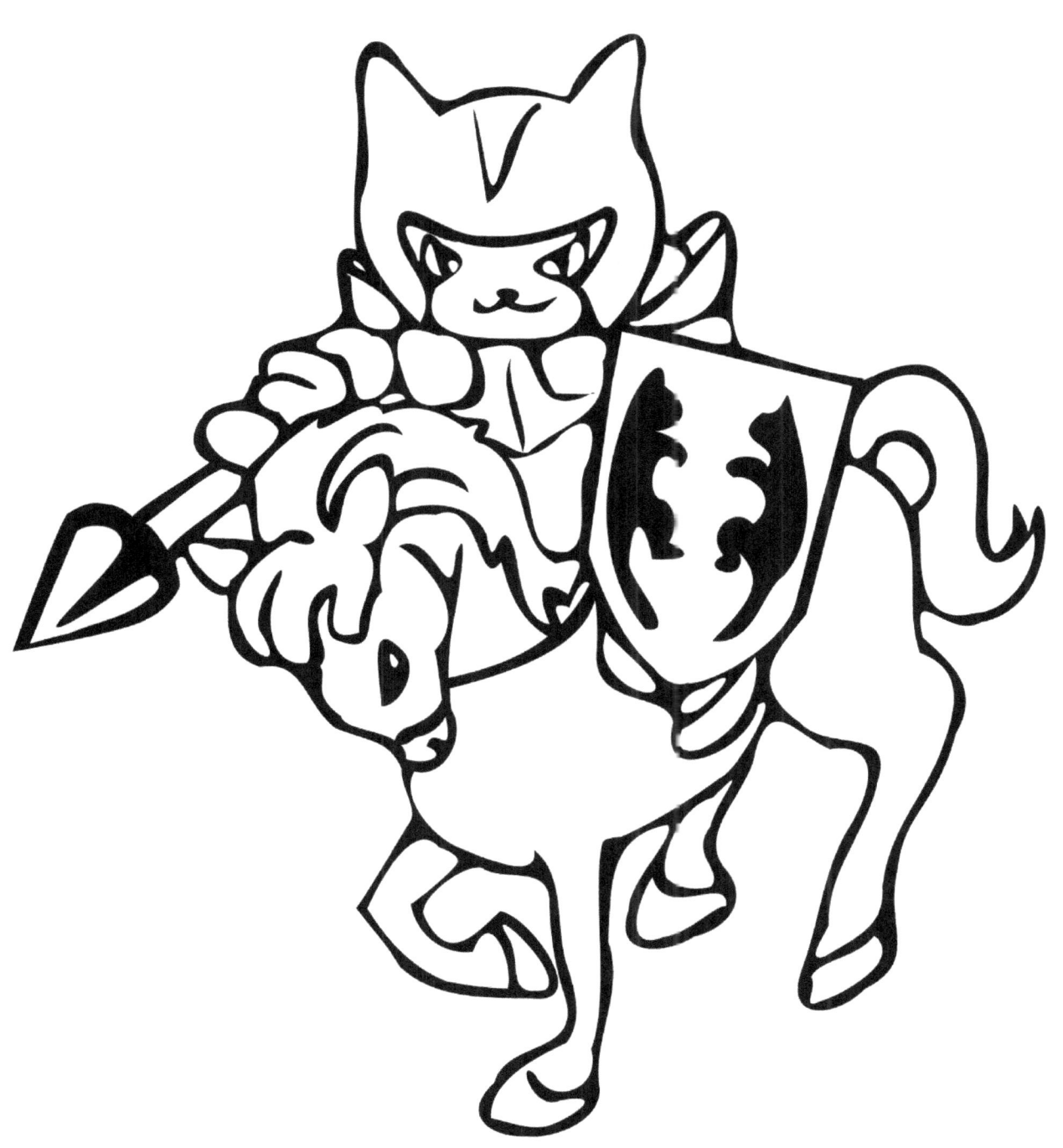

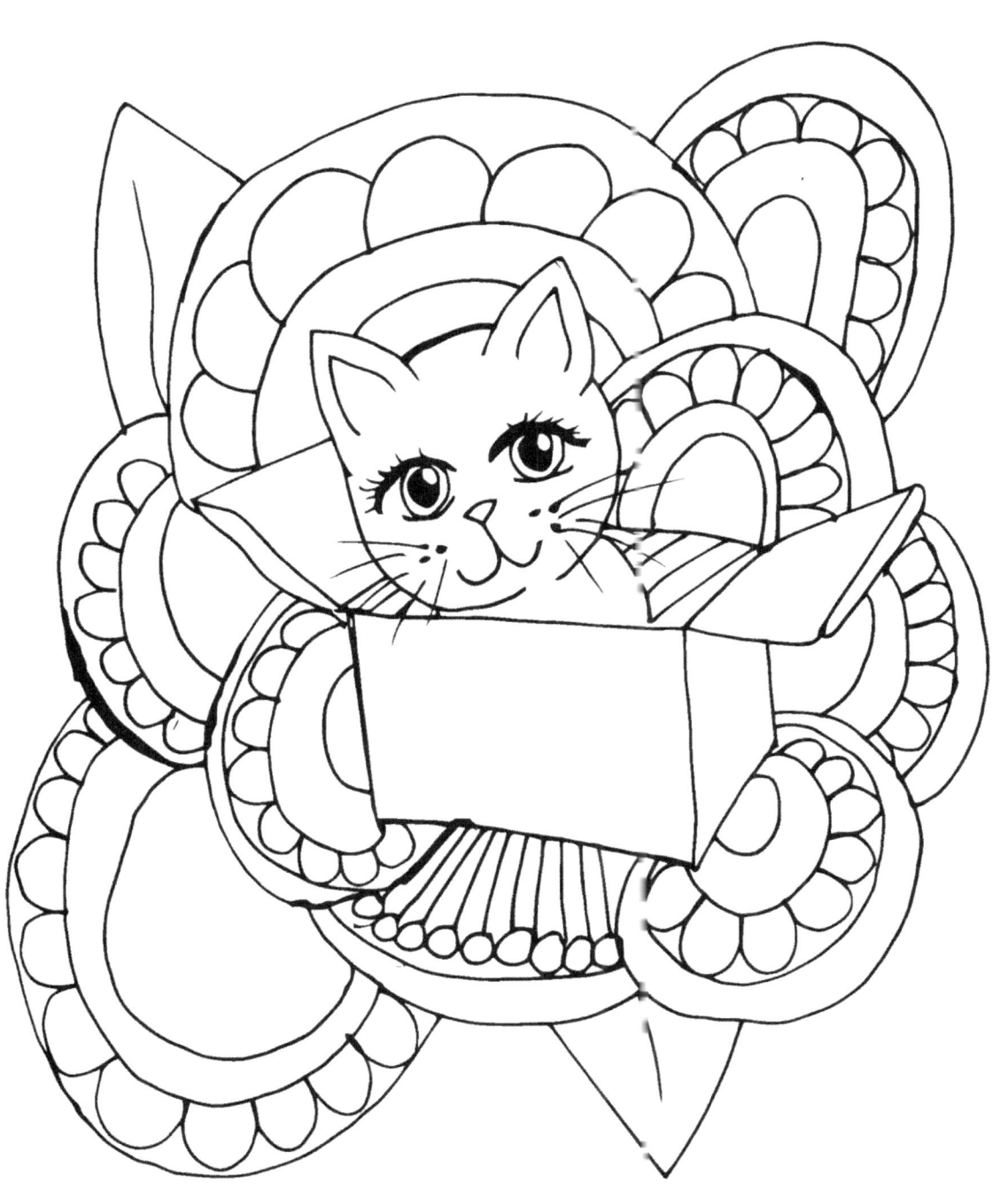

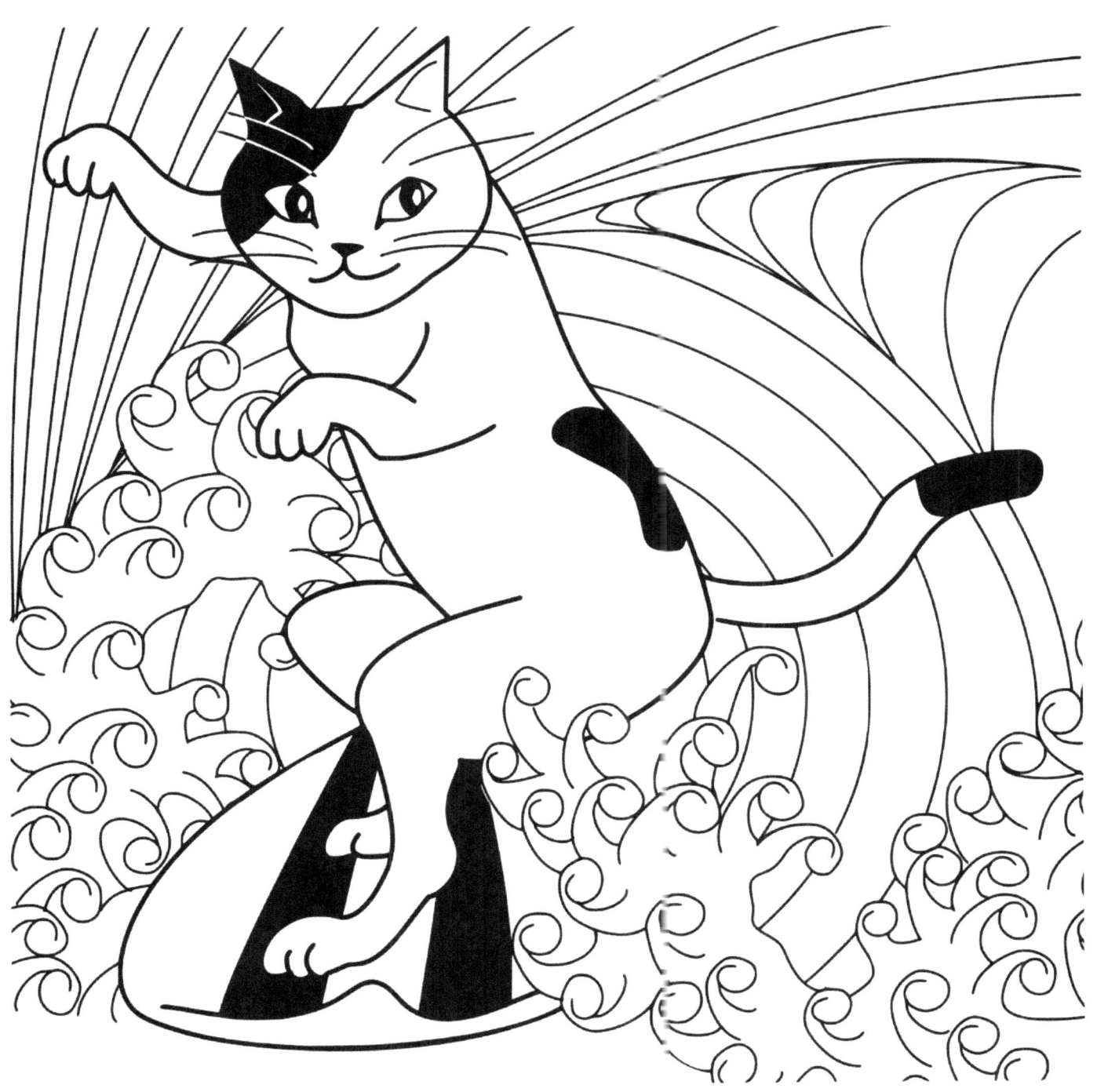

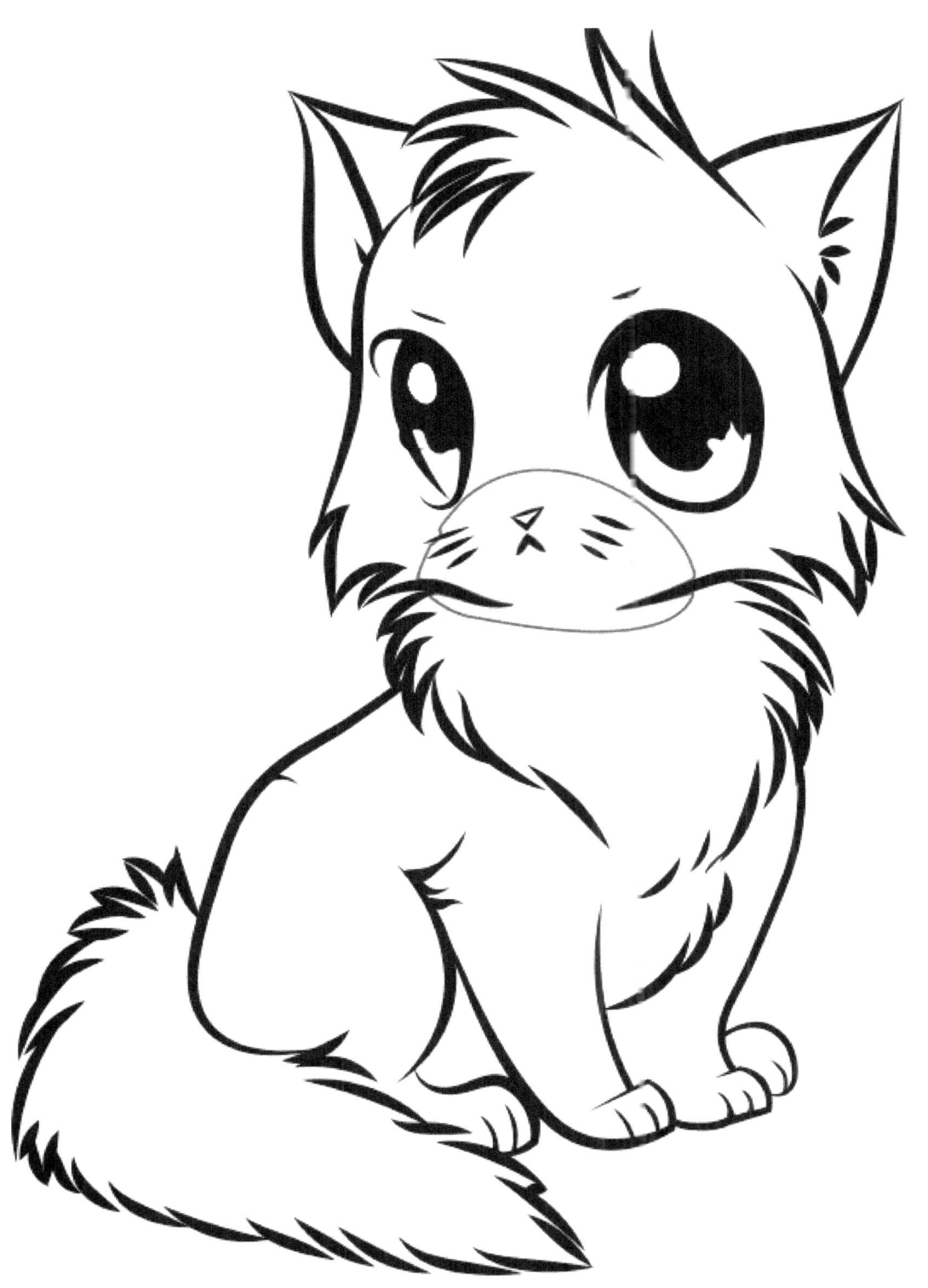

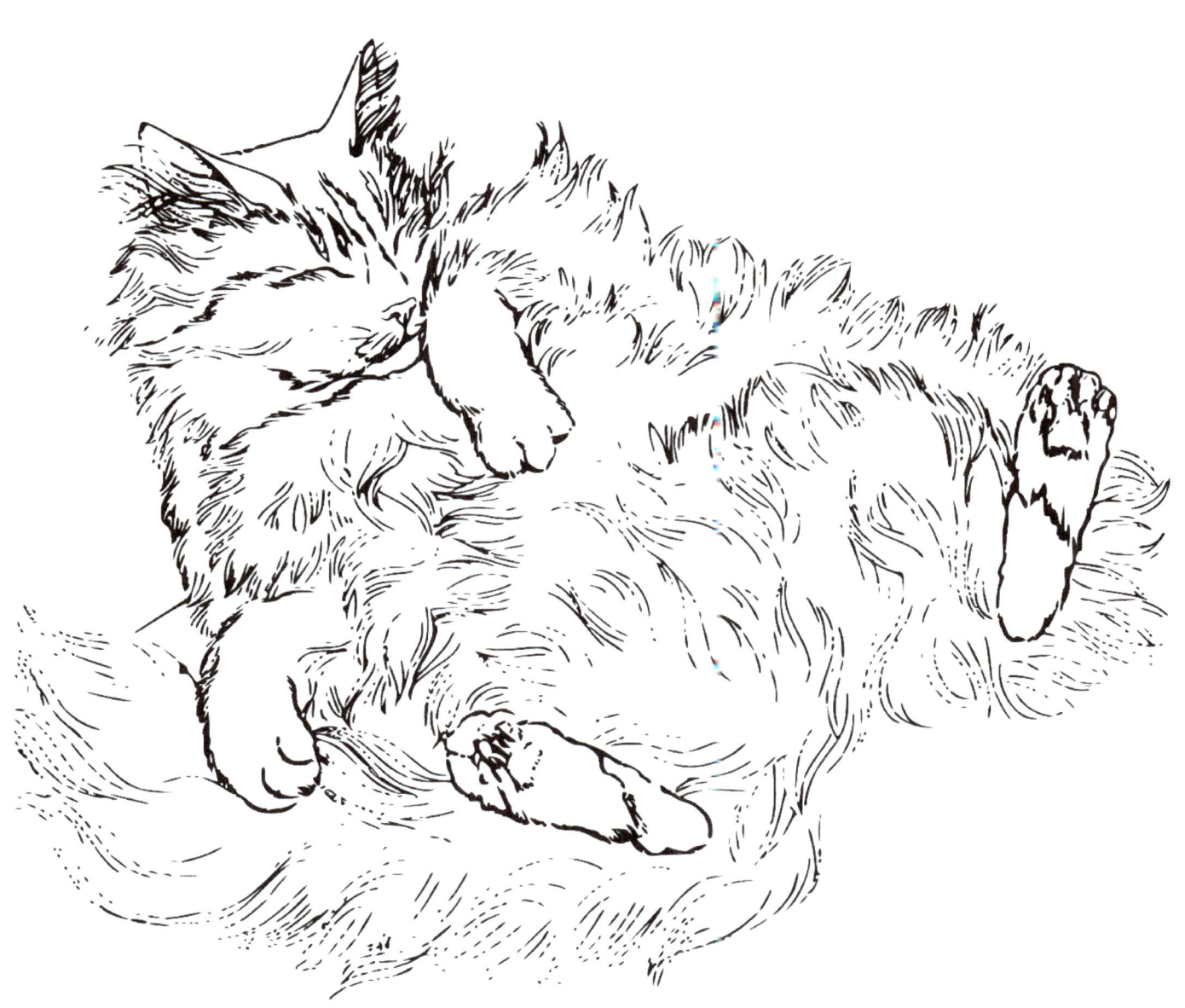

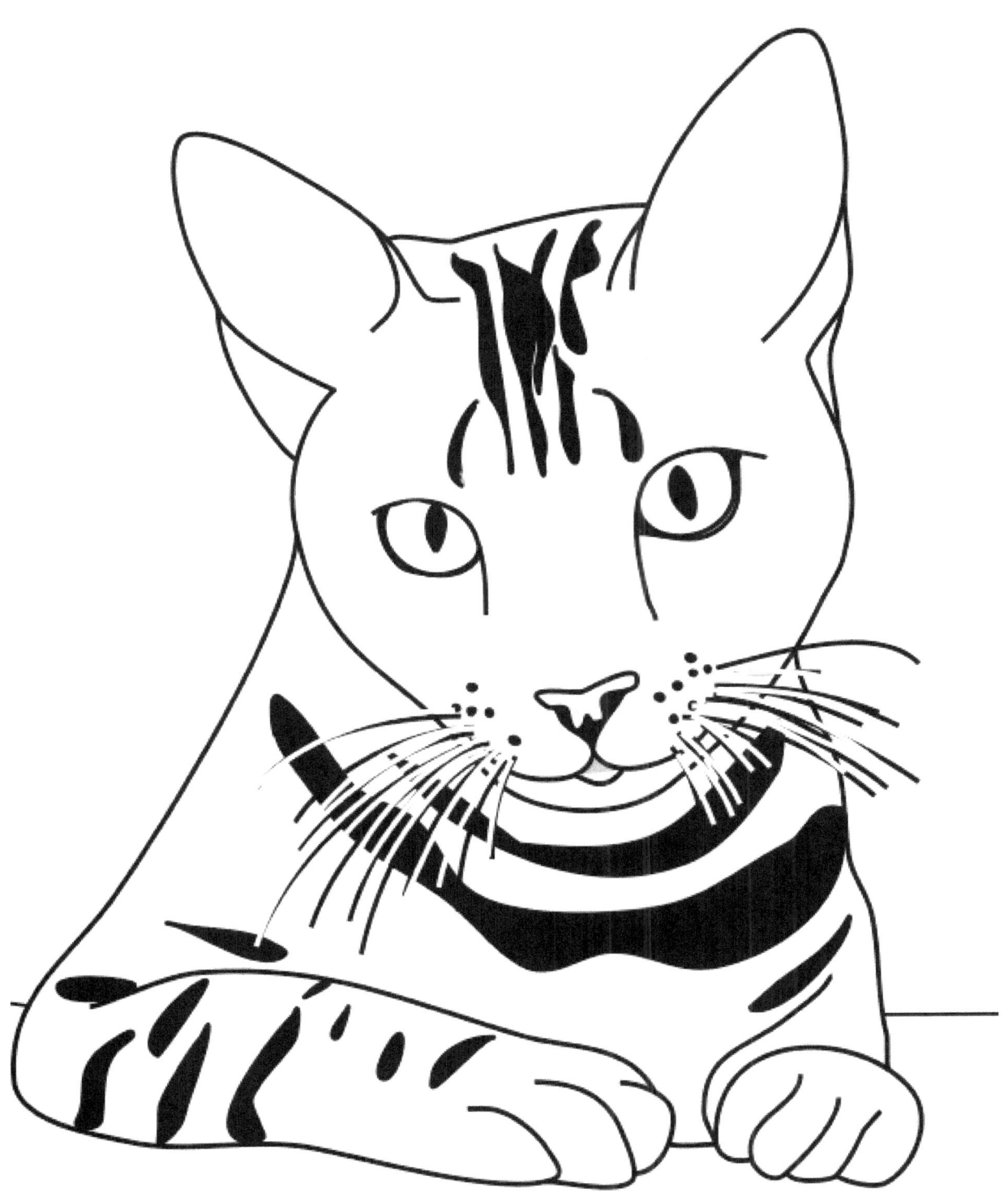

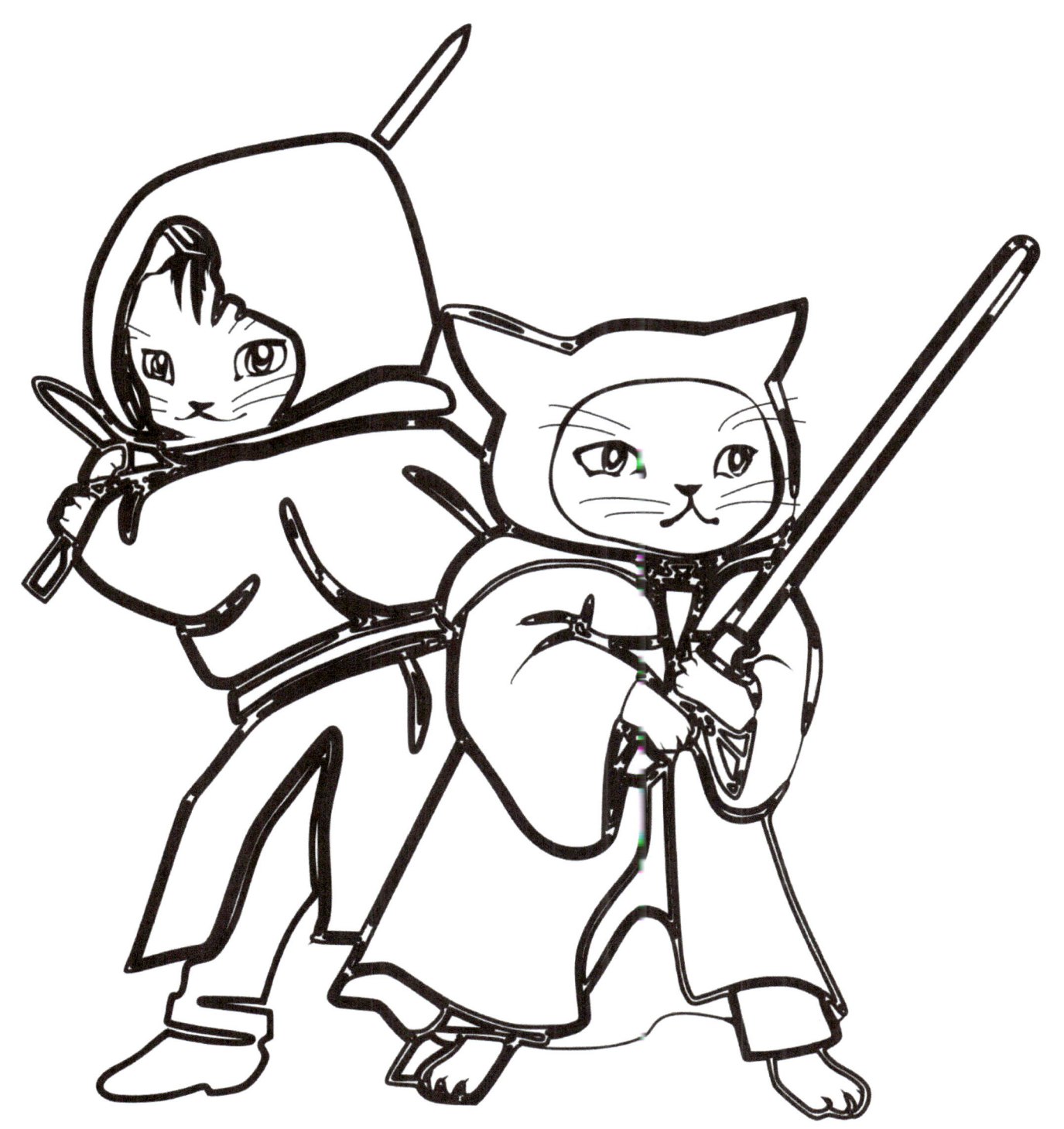

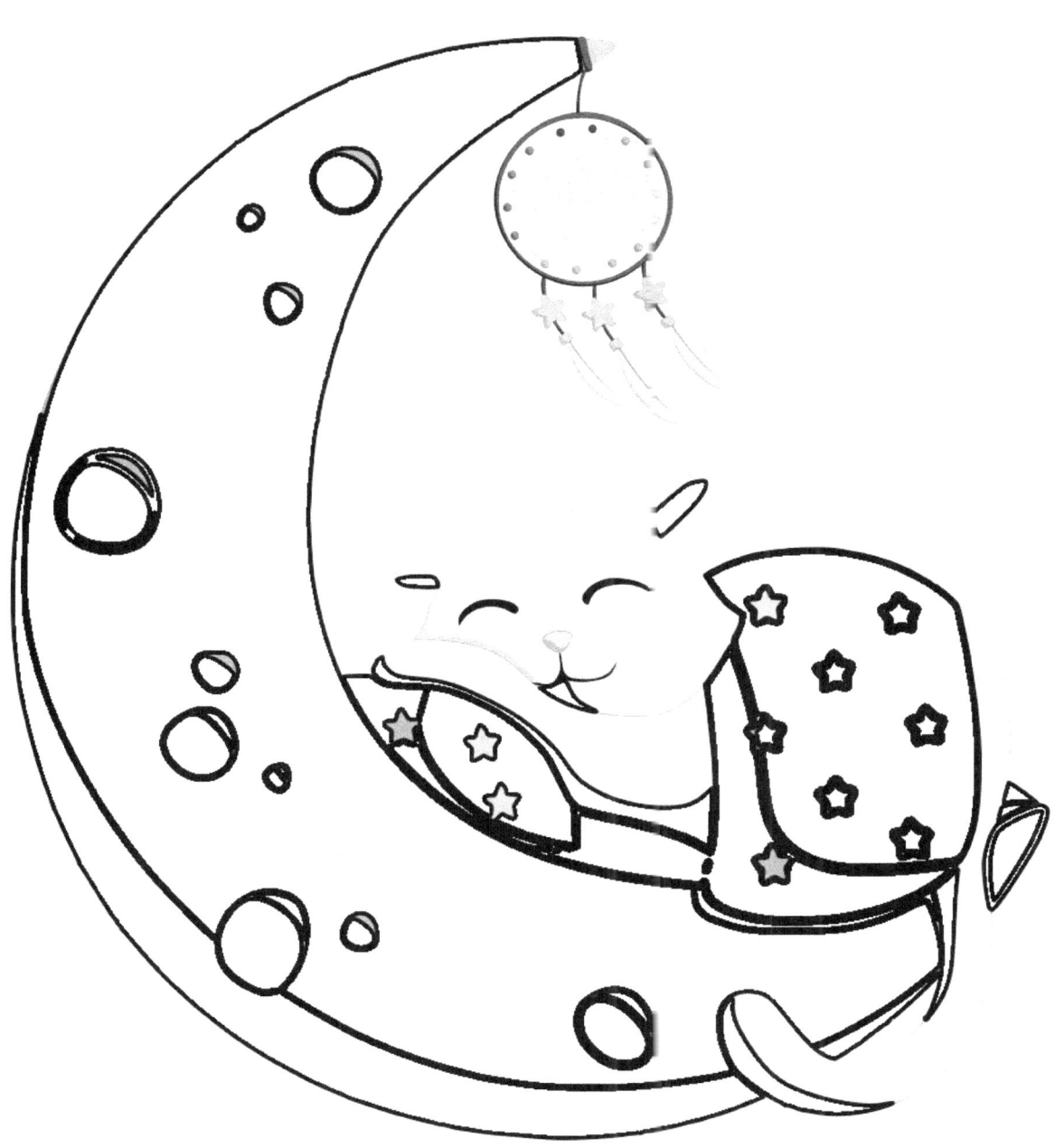

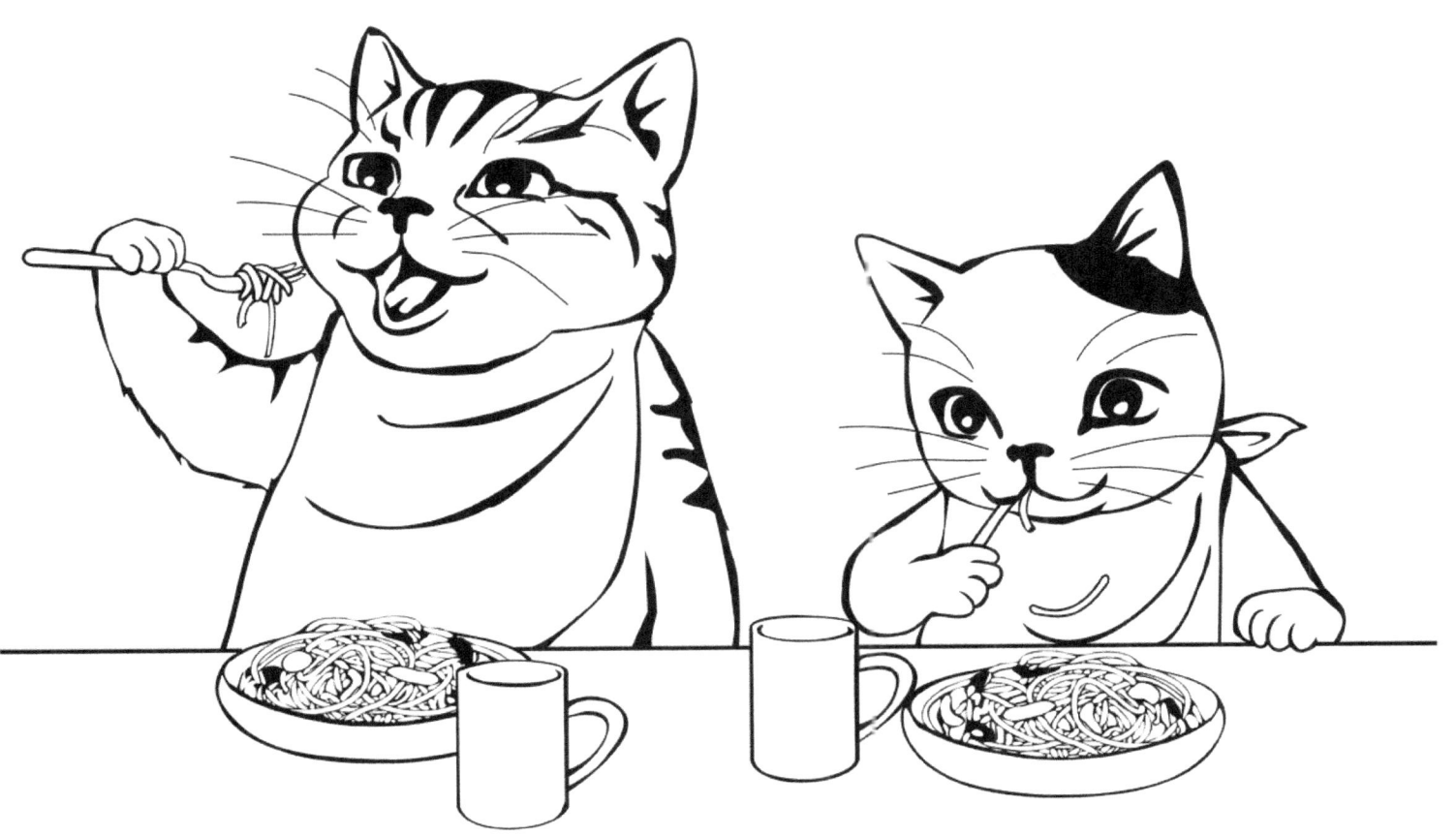

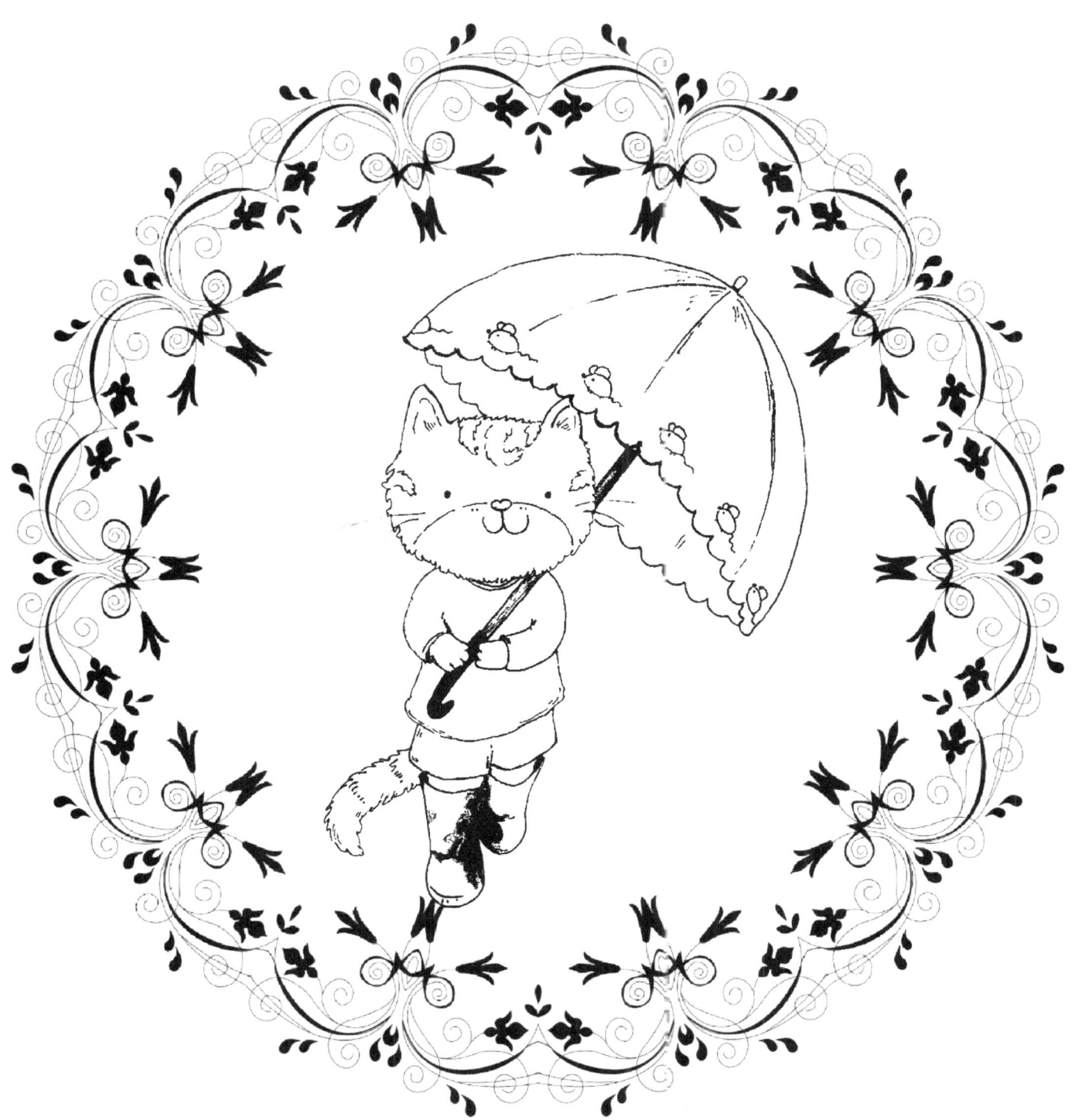

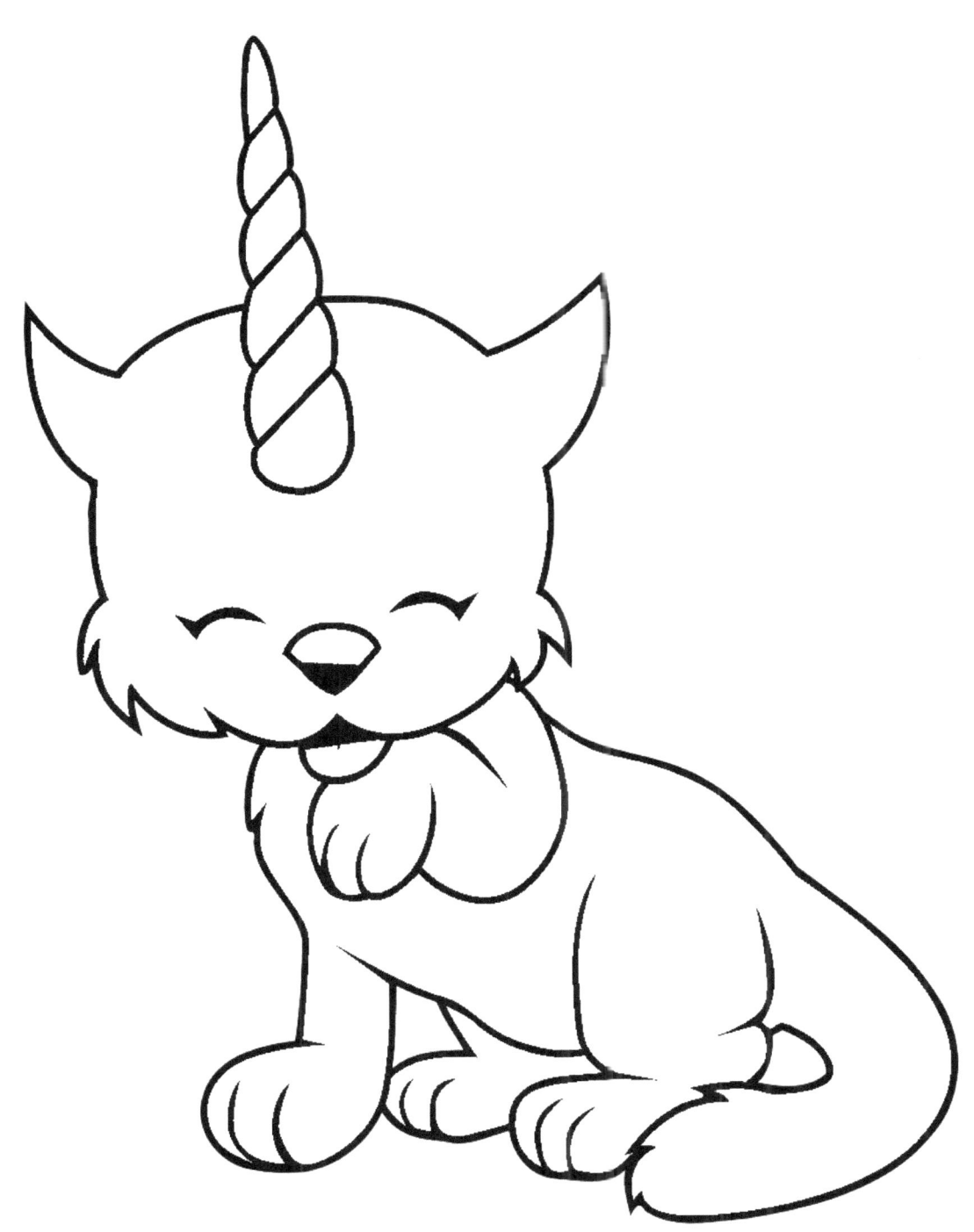

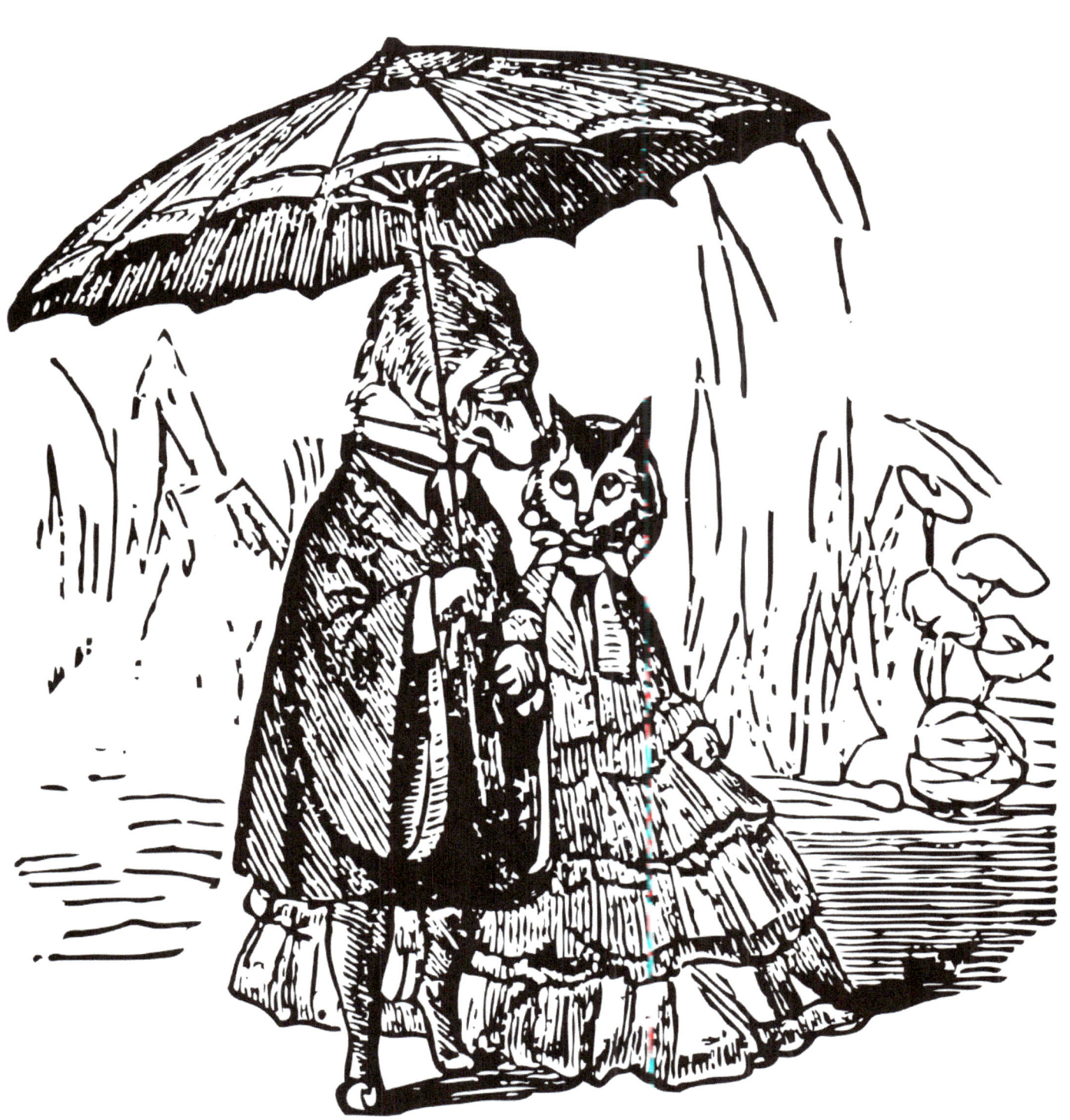

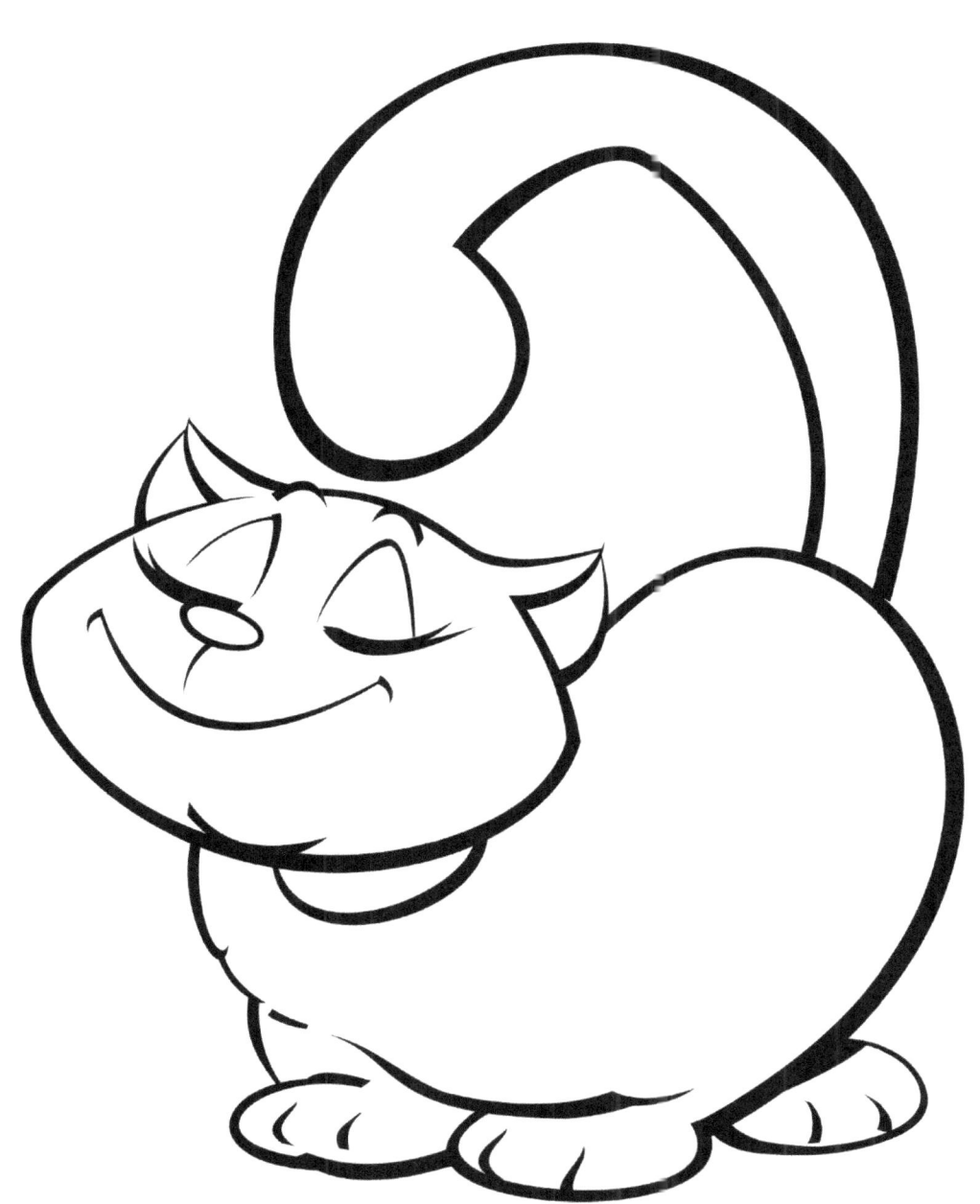

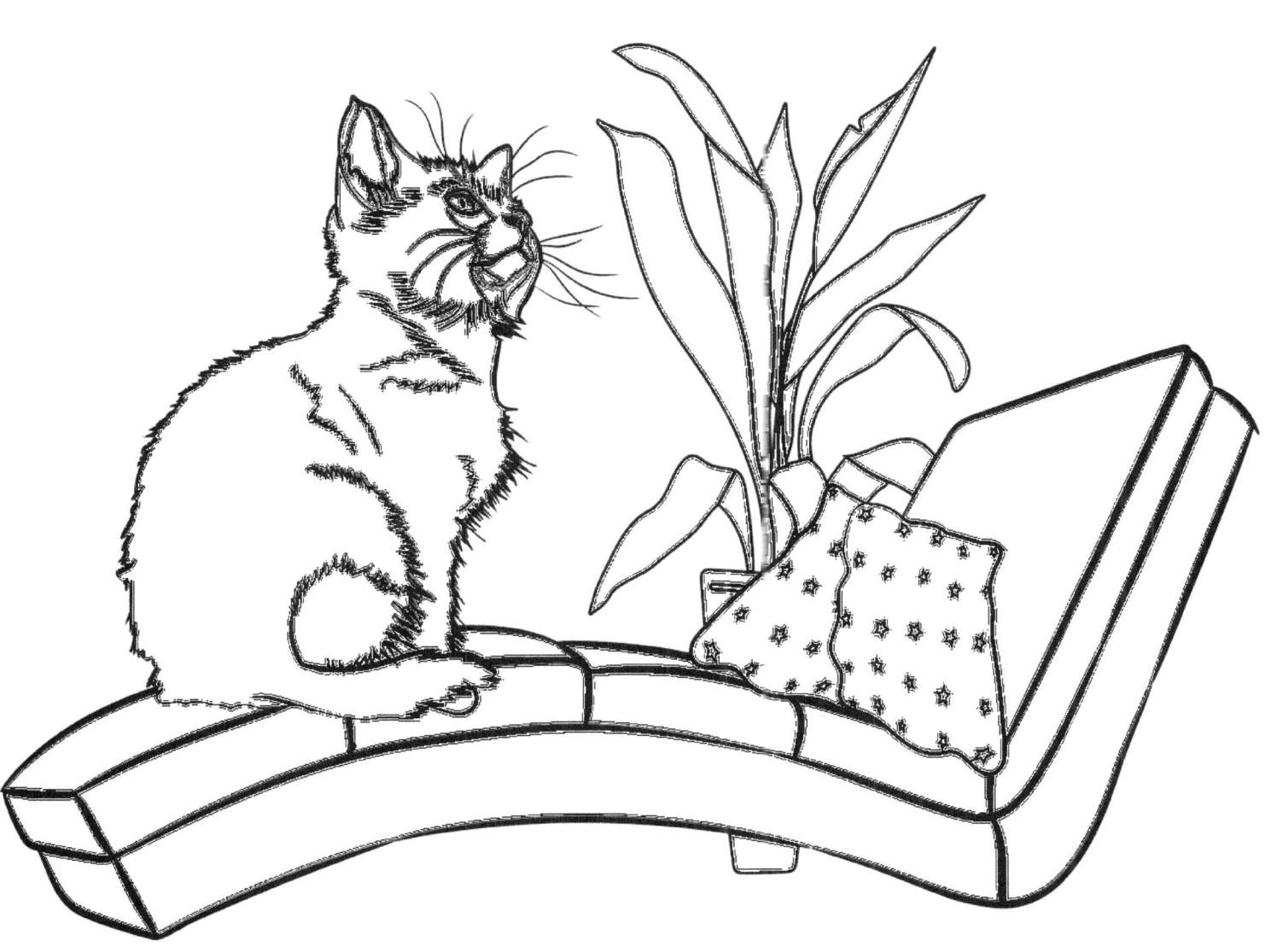

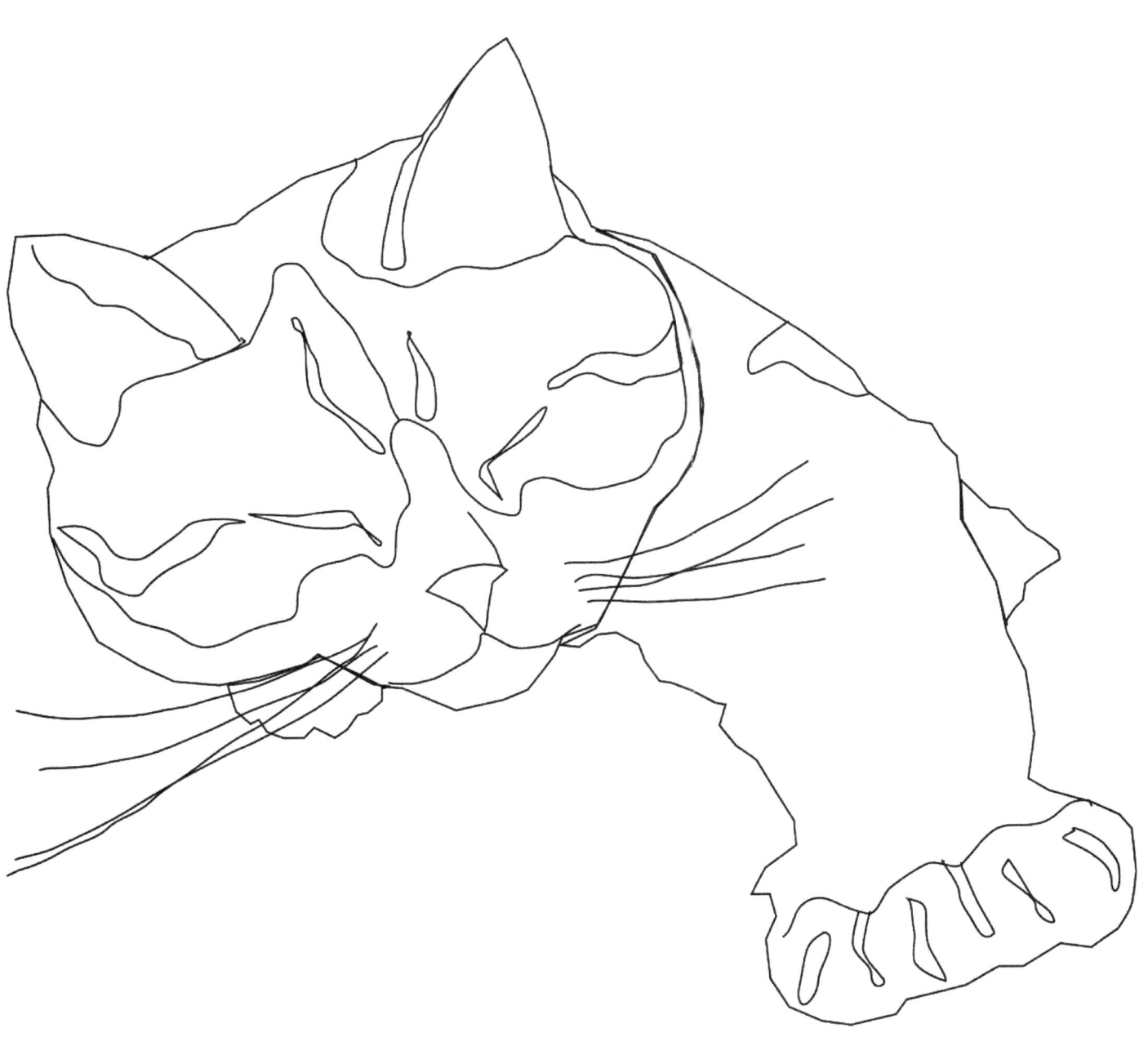

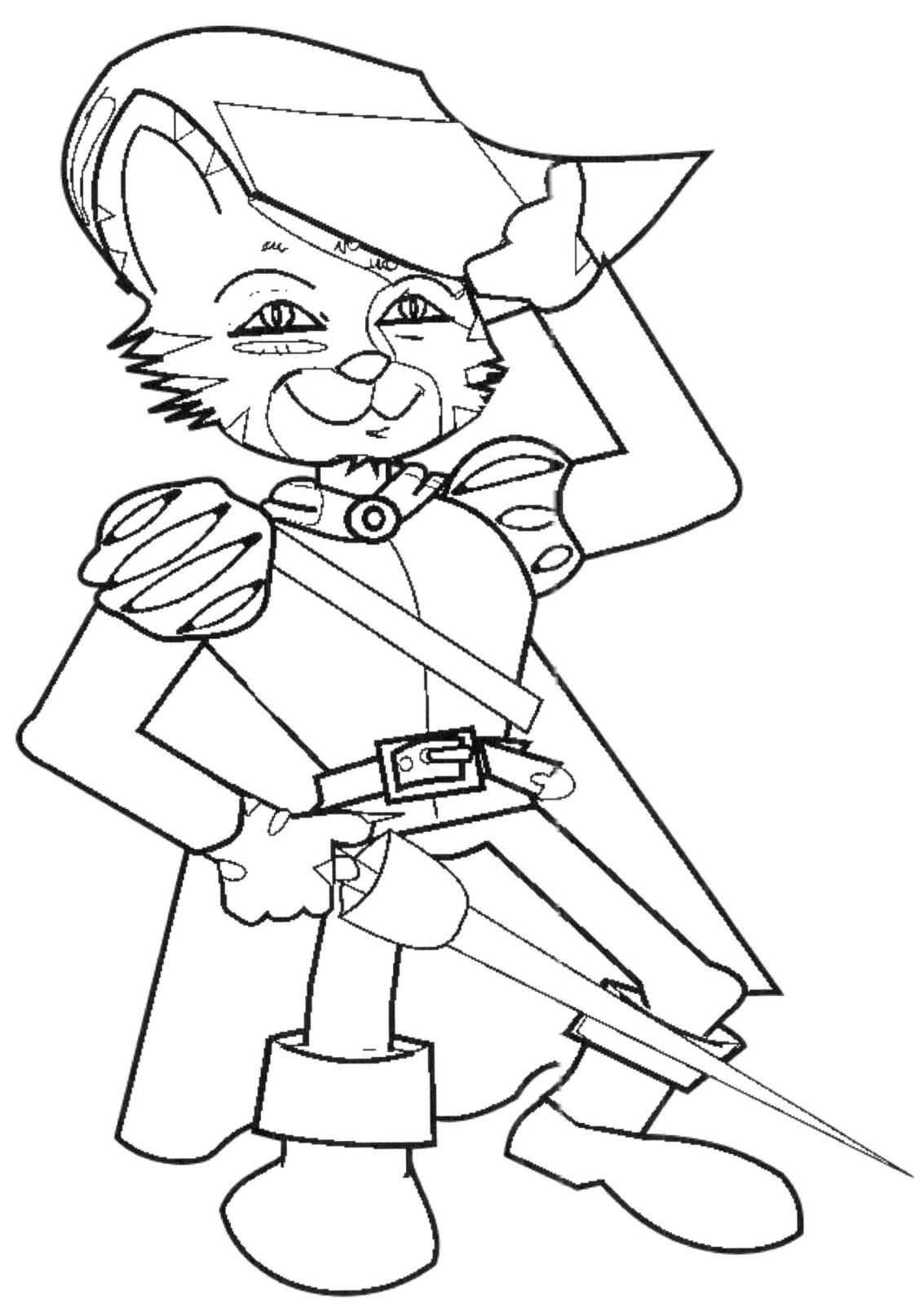

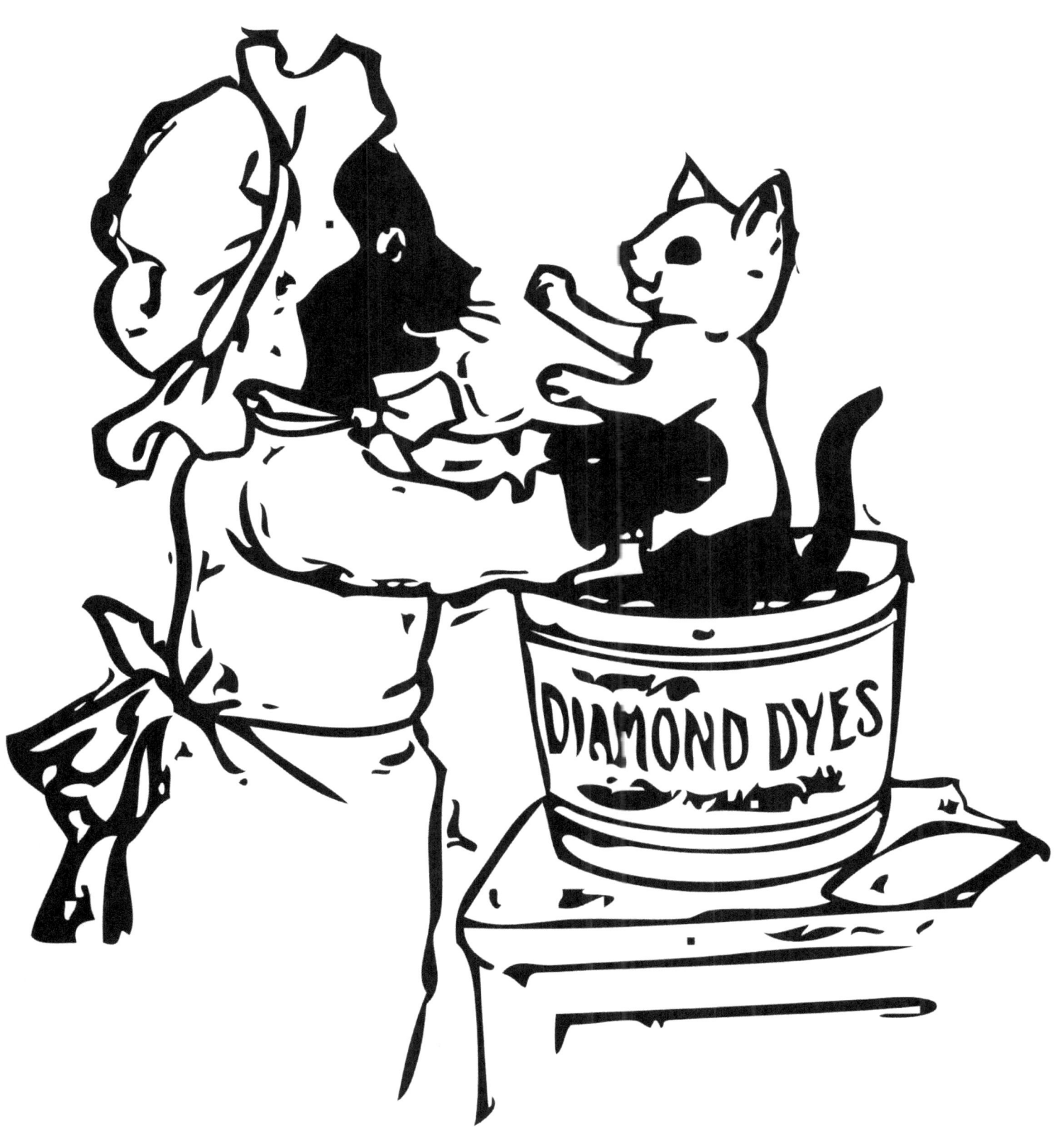

www.ingramcontent.com/pod-product-compliance
Lightning Source LLC
Chambersburg PA
CBHW060436220526
45465CB00008B/3157